REAL SOLUTIONS
for Getting Out of Debt

REAL SOLUTIONS
for Getting Out of Debt

Mike Yorkey

SERVANT PUBLICATIONS
ANN ARBOR, MICHIGAN

Vine Books is an imprint of Servant Publications especially designed to serve
evangelical Christians.

Servant Publications—Mission Statement

We are dedicated to publishing books that spread the gospel of Jesus
Christ, help Christians to live in accordance with that gospel, promote
renewal in the church, and bear witness to Christian unity.

Unless otherwise noted, Scripture verses are taken from The Living Bible.
Copyright 1971. Used by permission of Tyndale House Publishers, Inc.,
Wheaton, IL 60198. All rights reserved.

Scripture verses marked NIV are taken from the HOLY BIBLE, NEW INTER-
NATIONAL VERSION®. Copyright 1973,1978, 1984, by International Bible
Society. Used by permission of Zondervan Publishing House. All rights
reserved.

Although the men and women whose stories are told in this book are real,
all names have been changed or first names only have been used to protect
the privacy of those involved.

Published by Servant Publications
P.O. Box 8617
Ann Arbor, Michigan 48107
www.servantpub.com

Cover design: UDG DesignWorks, Portland, Ore.

02 03 04 05 10 9 8 7 6 5 4 3 2 1

Printed in the United States of America
ISBN 1-56955-340-8

Library of Congress Cataloging-in-Publication Data

Yorkey, Mike.
    Real solutions for getting out of debt / Mike Yorkey.
        p. cm.
    ISBN 1-56955-340-8 (alk. paper)
    1. Finance, Personal. 2. Consumer credit. 3. Debt. I. Title.
    HG179 .Y64 2002
    332.024'02–dc21

                                                          2002000883

DEDICATION

To my children, Andrea and Patrick
Don't get fooled by easy credit.

CONTENTS

I was originally asked by Bert Ghezzi of Servant Publications if I would be interested in writing *Real Solutions for Getting Out of Debt* several months before a band of terrorists commandeered four jet airliners on September 11, 2001.

At the time I politely declined his entreaty because I didn't feel any sense of urgency regarding the topic. Since I didn't feel any sense of urgency about debt and money woes, I figured that most Americans felt the same way. Times were good, weren't they?

Oh, there were a few cracks in the foundation prior to September 11. The U.S. economy had definitely slowed for the first time in ten years, which is why President George W. Bush pushed so hard for a "stimulus package" that included tax rebates and lower income tax rates. The slight economic downturn would be just a blip on the screen, predicted the pundits, the same ones who proclaimed the start of the New Economy during the 1990s. They said we were living in a unique time when our financial futures never burned brighter, thanks to computerized efficiencies and the dawn of the Internet Age. Drunk with high-flying stock prices and higher wages, one can make a general observation that we had become fat and lazy—spendaholics who were maxing out our credit cards with little regard for the future.

And then American Airlines Flight 11, with Mohammed Atta at the controls, slammed into the south tower of the World

Trade Center. When the Twin Towers imploded in Lower Manhattan within minutes of the Pentagon taking a direct hit from another American Airlines plane, everything about our American society changed. The terrorists, whose bloodthirsty acts were prompted by a desire to kill tens of thousands on the ground, hoped to topple the U.S. economy as well.

Time will tell how successful they were, but the attacks of September 11 destroyed our sense of invulnerability. Shortly after the attack, I read an essay by Peggy Noonan, a columnist with *The Wall Street Journal,* that was published in *Forbes* magazine back in November 1998. Ms. Noonan's observations from several years ago are eerily prescient when read in the context of post–September 11. "History has handed us one of the easiest rides in all the story of man," she began. "It has handed us a wave of wealth so broad and so deep that it would be almost disorienting if we thought about it a lot, which we don't."

I heartily agreed with Peggy. I remember thinking a similar thought during a trans-Atlantic flight a few years ago. I was coming home from a family trip to Switzerland, and as I gazed at the whitecaps churning the North Sea from thirty-nine thousand feet, I marveled at how I was going to sleep in my bed on the California coastline *that night.* It wasn't that long ago—just 150 years—that it took *months* to travel from Zurich to San Diego, if you survived the harrowing trans-Atlantic voyage by boat and a dangerous overland trip by wagon train.

Peggy made a second great point regarding how good life had been in the United States at this moment in history. "Lately this leaves me uneasy," she wrote. "Does it you? Do you wonder how and why exactly we have it so different, so nice compared to thousands of years of peasants eating rocks? Only three generations ago, my family had to sweat in the sun to pull food from the ground."

And now we wring our hands in frustration if the microwave goes on the fritz. I say all this to state that our pampered generation is living in a new reality—a reality of declining jobs, a contracting economy, and a possible deflation in home prices. While all these economic indicators concern me, the one that causes shivers to run up and down my spine is the *huge* increase in household credit card debt. In 1990, the average American family carried $2,985 in credit card debt. A little more than ten years later, that number (according to CardWeb.com) has ballooned to $8,562 per household—a stunning 186 percent increase!

It's obvious that we are living beyond our means, which leads me to why I'm writing *Real Solutions for Getting Out of Debt*. If I can help a few families keep their financial boats from going over the falls, then I will consider this book a success. Let me complete the word picture here. Life should be like riding a canoe down a slow, meandering river of life. When you have manageable debt—a reasonable home mortgage and modest car payments—then it can be said that the river is moving languidly downstream. It's at moments like these that you have time to drink in the beauty of the passing countryside: the deer walking along the riverbank; the spring flowers bursting forth amid the dewy grasslands; and tall, stately firs that threaten to touch the sky.

But when you pile on more and more credit card debt, your financial river starts moving faster and faster. Not only do you *not* have time to watch the scenery pass by—to enjoy life—but you have to be on the lookout for furious stretches of white water. You never know when rapids are going to appear.

And then the unexpected happens—a job layoff or a "reassignment" to a lower-paying position. The family income takes a hit, and suddenly, you're buffeted to and fro, spending more and more money on the credit cards without any way of paying back more than the minimum amount. You're stressed by the mounting pressure. You're bothered by creditors and hassled by lenders. As you move swiftly down the stream, you can hear the roar of Bankruptcy Falls in the distance. If you don't get off the fast-flow river of debt soon, you're going to go over the falls!

I don't want that to happen to you. Nearly two hundred years ago, Charles Dickens wrote something in his book *David Copperfield* that reminds us spending more than we earn is nothing new under the sun. "Annual income twenty pounds, annual expenditure nineteen nineteen six, result happiness," wrote Dickens. "Annual income twenty pounds, annual expenditure twenty pounds ought and six, result misery."

In other words, spending less money than you have in your pocket equals happiness, but spending more than you take in equals misery.

But, Mike, I don't feel miserable at all! I can afford these things. It's okay to have some debt.

Yes, thanks to the ubiquitous credit card, you can afford to buy almost anything your heart desires—a shiny new car (many dealers accept Visa!), a Caribbean vacation, or a night on the town. Those things can make us happy, and I've enjoyed all those materials things as well. But if you're not careful about the way money leaves your fingers, not tracking how much debt you're piling up, then you could become very miserable someday, and you won't be able to spend your way out of your misery.

Tight Margin

I identify a great deal with Charles Dickens' quotation because some years it feels as though I've earned twenty pounds and spent "twenty ought six." On those occasions, we had to withdraw savings from past years to make up the shortfall. Other years we managed to spend "nineteen nineteen six," which made me happy, but there sure wasn't much left over to replenish our meager savings accounts, and I can prove it. When a half dozen years ago I started tracking our family finances on Quicken, a financial software program, I learned that the Yorkey family spent 97.2 percent of everything that came in, which was just one more reminder that our family was one car breakdown away from going over the edge.

Life has been a battle for us, as I'm sure it has been for you as well. Our family's toughest moments came when I was working for a start-up editorial company in 1998. I had left *Focus on the Family* magazine and uprooted my family from Colorado Springs to San Diego because my parents still lived there, and I missed the mild Mediterranean climate of my youth. Within four months at my new job, the paychecks stopped, however, and I didn't know what to do.

We were in the middle of an escrow on a home that my wife, Nicole, and I believe that God led us to (which is another long story). Mortgage lenders tend to prefer making home loans to people who are gainfully employed. Since there was the promise of "we'll get you caught up" at my work, I continued to show up at my new job, figuring that if I helped turn around the company, then I had a better chance to receive back pay.

Meanwhile, I closed escrow and took out a first trust deed for $15,000 more to tide us through the tough times. I worked four and a half months without a paycheck before finally deciding that I could no longer contribute to a fantasy world where the employees work for free. I went home and started my freelance writing career.

Looking back, the only way we made it was by the grace of God's people (we were financially blessed by friends in miraculous, incredible ways) and a dogged determination not to take on any more debt besides our home mortgage. That meant driving well-used cars (wait until you hear about those) and paying off our credit card statements in full each month (more miracles), continuing a practice that Nicole and I had done since we were married in 1979.

Having stayed out of debt, I fear that we will be going *into* debt because my two teenagers have reached the college years. Starting with the fall of 2002, Andrea and Patrick plan to attend private Christian colleges, which cost around $20,000 a year *each*. Don't get me wrong. Sending your children to a Christian college is a wonderful problem to have, and I'm not complaining at all. I will not mind taking on new debt (such as student loans or an equity line of credit) to help make that happen because I think Christian education is that important.

But my kids' education is where I will draw the line in the sand; I'm not going to get a second mortgage so Nicole and I can go heli-skiing in the Bugaboos. That's why it's my belief that too many American families are paddling in rapidly moving waters. If you feel that you are in that boat, then stick with me. You'll be shown how to determine how fast the financial river is moving, what steps you can take to slow down the spending river, and how to steer away from Bankruptcy Falls if you have accumulated too much credit card debt.

Background Story

Before we begin in earnest, you should know a little about my background. For more than eleven years, I was editor of *Focus on the Family* magazine, a monthly periodical mailed to two million homes each month. When it came to deciding what type of stories should go into the magazine, my heart was attuned to the financial struggles that families were going through, especially in Christian homes where Mom was staying home to raise the children because both parents thought that was the best way to instill godly values in their kids. The decision to keep Mom at home comes at a price (believe me, I knew since that's what Nicole and I were doing), so I was open to publishing articles that helped families with their finances.

This interest led me to write a book for Servant called *Saving Money Any Way You Can*, which helped families look for ways to save their hard-earned cash on everyday purchases and major expenditures such as automobiles, appliances, and summer vacations. That book was well received in the marketplace when it came out about eight years ago, and now I'm pleased that Servant has asked me to tackle the topic of staying out of debt.

Times could get very tough in the wake of 9/11. We are in the midst of our first recession in ten years, ending a record-breaking economic expansion when times were truly good. The National Bureau of Economic Research says that we are in our tenth recession since World War II, but many of those recessions happened in the late 1940s and 1950s. That's ancient history to today's young families, who have never experienced a falling economy as adults, complete with layoffs and wage stagnation.

In our family, the current recession has certainly caused me to bring out my worry beads. Since 1998, Nicole and I have ridden a roller coaster of emotions, wondering how we will get that Visa bill paid (we have just one credit card). Somehow, we've managed to do it, but I've certainly acted like Chief Worrier leading up to the due date. What has helped keep me relatively calm are Jesus' words from Matthew 6: "So my counsel is this: Don't worry about things—food, drink, and clothes. For you already have life and a body—and they are far more important than what to eat and wear. Look at the birds! They don't worry about what to eat—for your heavenly Father feeds them. And you are far more valuable to him than they are" (25-26).

Nope, I don't have too much to worry about, and neither do you. But that doesn't absolve us from doing our part to spend wisely and doing our best to avoid the debt trap. To help you in that effort, the first part of *Real Solutions for Getting Out of Debt* will talk about the major steps you can take to cut expenses and stave off some form of loan consolidation. For those of you who've exhausted your savings, who've maxed out your credit cards, and who don't see a way out of your financial mess, I will share how you can right your listing financial ship in chapter nine, where I talk about how credit counselors work with you to formulate a debt repayment plan and act as middlemen between you and your creditors.

Let's roll up our sleeves and get started.

ONE

Like on Wings of a Bird

Call us old-fashioned, but Nicole and I share a single check-book. I think we do things that way because I don't want the daunting challenge of balancing two checkbooks each month. Sharing a checkbook has also taught me that Nicole doesn't pay much attention to the far right side of the checkbook ledger, the part where you write in the check amount and subtract it from the remaining balance.

Maybe that's because it's difficult to deduct a $134.60 check made out to Costco when the line above it has $89.42 inscribed there. At any rate, because Nicole is mathematically challenged in this area, I've learned to periodically peek at the checkbook (since Nicole carries it in her purse) to see whether it needs a "fill-up."

There are times when I wish I owned a gas station because our fill-ups seem to last as long as a drive around the block. The old saying "We're spending it as fast it comes in" certainly applies to our family, as I'm sure it does for yours. I was relatively clueless regarding how quickly our money was flying out the window in the first ten years of our marriage until I began noticing in the late 1980s how Nicole and I were steadily raiding our savings account to make up for shortfalls. You could call them our "fill-ups."

Sure, we paid all our bills and never carried a credit card balance, but that strategy eroded any hard-won reserves. Simply put, we were spending more than we were taking in— not a whole lot, but just enough. I guess that's what I figured "savings" were for.

At that time, we had just purchased our first home, a thirty-year-old tract model that was begging for a few home-improvement projects, such as adding automatic sprinklers, ripping up the shabby linoleum in the kids' bathroom, and hauling an old rock garden to the dump. We learned that aging tract homes can be money pits, too, just like those fancy new homes at Villagio. Our savings account began shrinking like a cotton shirt left in the dryer too long. If something wasn't done, we were headed for financial trouble.

With only a vague awareness of what I was doing, I decided to do a year-end accounting of the in-go and out-go. This was 1989, a time when we didn't own one of those newfangled "personal computers" that everyone seemed to be talking about; I would have to do our personal finances by hand. I hauled out a spiral notebook and divided the pages into categories. I found my checkbook ledger, credit card statements, and various cash receipts in a shoebox and began tallying what we had purchased over the last year. I wanted to know how much we spent on the American Dream of owning a home: mortgage, property taxes, and home insurance. Then I devoted pages to groceries, restaurants, automotive costs (gas and repair bills), medical expenses, vacations, and any-thing else I could think of.

This was a lot of work in those pre-PC days! Finally, after a long weekend, I was confronted with the awful truth: we had spent $2,534 *more* than we had taken in during 1989. We had dipped into savings to cover the shortfall.

I shared my "profit and loss" report with Nicole over dinner at our favorite Chinese restaurant. I figured I had to sugar her up for the belt-tightening ahead, and she took it well. The following year, I'm happy to report, we came out $1,141 ahead. In the intervening years, we've managed to stay in the black *most* of the time. I know you were expecting me to say that following our epiphany Nicole and I had our financial act totally together, that we had become a couple who zealously watched over our expenditures in our right hand to see whether they matched up with our ironclad family budget in our left hand.

Fat chance. We are just like you, muddling through, somehow keeping the bills paid. For all the ups and downs, however, I feel that we have managed a tremendous victory in not taking on any additional debt. I don't make this statement to be proud but more as recognition of the Lord's provision, of a desire to listen to good advice, and of an ambition not to do anything stupid.

Frankly, our family finances have been a miracle. This full-time "author gig" that I have going has resulted in wild fluctuations of income, meaning that we've had to rely on savings to see us through during those months when no checks come in. But we have managed to stay on top of our bills, credit card statements, and the kids' expensive private school tuition, although doing so has been the toughest task we've ever tackled.

A Passion for Families

I may be going out on a limb here, but I have a sneaky feeling that you're reading this book because you are in some kind of debt.

Before we go any further, let me put all the cards on the table. I am not a financial counselor, and I've never had any desire to be one. I took one accounting class in college and vowed to never get near a balance sheet again in my life. I've honored that promise I made to myself.

What I do bring to the table is a passion for families—and their predicaments. Following my time with *Focus on the Family* magazine, I went out on my own as a writer, which included a yearlong stint as the content editor of atFamilies.com, a family-related web site. Working for a Christian ministry, for an Internet start-up, and for myself as an itinerate writer ("Will write for food") has given me a great education since I read and edit dozens of books and articles relating to family finances.

One of the books that left a deep impression is *Margin: Restoring Emotional, Physical, Financial, and Time Reserves to Overloaded Lives* by Richard A. Swenson, a Christian doctor who saw a steady stream of exhausted, hurting people coming into his office. Many of these patients were sick because they couldn't handle the stress of financial pressures, which Dr. Swenson called "overload." His prescription: building margin into our lives.

Going through life without margin is like being thirty minutes late for your son's basketball game because you were twenty minutes late getting out of a meeting because you were ten minutes late getting back from lunch. Going through life without financial margin is worrying whether you are one car breakdown away from maxing out your credit cards. Going through life *with* margin means establishing parameters that leave extra money at the end of the month. For some people, this could be something as simple as buying a used Chrysler minivan for under $12,000 rather than leasing a shiny new Suburban that costs three times as much out the showroom door.

But we are getting ahead of ourselves here. Before you can start taking some proactive steps to stay out of debt, you need to know how heavy your financial burdens weigh.

Do you know where your family finances stand? How much debt do you owe? You would be surprised at the number of couples who have only a *vague* idea regarding how much debt they're saddled with. Many couples are afraid to seek out the answer—kind of like ignoring dizzy spells and the blood you're coughing up because you don't want to find out that you have cancer.

It shouldn't be that difficult to determine, however, because most families pile on debt through one financial avenue—the credit card (or multiple credit cards, I'm afraid), which reminds me of the old saying: *It's eleven o'clock. Do you know how much credit card debt you have?*

Well, do you? If so, and if you have a household income of between $25,000 and $100,000, then these are the debt numbers I think you should be paying attention to:

- **$2,500 or less.** This is a reasonable amount of credit card debt. Notice that I didn't say this is an *ideal* amount of debt since the ideal is none, but with a little discipline—scaling back a summer vacation, keeping the cars longer—this chunk can be wiped out in six to twelve months or right away with some windfall, like a tax refund.

- **$2,500 to $5,000.** Now is the time to be officially concerned. If you have this much credit card debt, I'm figuring that you've had it for a while. Perhaps when your credit card statement (or statements!) arrive, you shield your eyes from the balance and direct them to the part where it says "Minimum Payment Required." That's not good.

  Once the credit card debt passes the $2,500 barrier, it's pretty easy psychologically to let things go, and before you know it, you're pushing five figures. This is where you must nip this nasty debt in the bud.

- **$5,000 to $10,000.** This is not good news. If things don't get turned around in a hurry, then you are a certified spendaholic. You need a plan to get this paid off. If you don't, you could be headed down a track toward consolidation loans, which merely replace short-term debt with long-term debt.

- **$10,000 and up.** Well, you've pushed through a psychological barrier—the five-figure one—and broken on through to the other side. I hate to say it so starkly, but you and your family are in trouble. You are mortgaging your tomorrow because of profligate spending in the past.

Overspending is a tough habit to break, similar to walking past a Starbucks without stopping to purchase a café mocha, extra hot, nonfat milk, and no whip. The trick is to not walk in the direction of a Starbucks—to not even *go there*.

Please don't get me wrong. You don't have to strike Starbucks out of your life. I'm saying that you should look at cutting back on lattes and frappaccinos and eating out and three-day weekends at out-of-town resorts and all the "frills" that make life nice but, in a pinch, you could do without.

But, Mike, you're talking about my lifestyle!

I could be, and it's not easy to cut back on the niceties of life that we've grown accustomed to. But you're spending more than you're earning, and eventually something has to give. If you continue adding thousands of more dollars to your credit card balances, there will come a day when you can barely make the minimum payments. Not long after that, you won't be able to pay anything toward those credit cards because your money must pay for the essentials—mortgage (or rent), food, and utilities.

People who have been there before will tell you that a panicky feeling of desperation never left their throat. The constant worry sapped their mental energies. They experienced a physical listlessness. I want to help you spare yourself this modern-day scourge of credit card debt. Adding up what you owe is the first step toward determining what you will do next.

Where the Winds Are Blowing

As you start adding up your consumer debt, this is also the time to start tracking your expenses, a task that I recommend continuing until you burn your mortgage. Tracking your expenses will not only tell you more clearly where you stand, but it will highlight areas where you're spending too much— like take-home pizza. What tracking expenses does is give you a big-picture sense of the State of Your Financial Union. Then if you get hit with a bigger-than-usual bill—a $700 car repair bill, for instance—you'll know it's time to cut back in other areas.

Fortunately, you don't have to use an old spiral notebook as I did years ago. Since I figure that your household has a computer (used ones can be had for just a few hundred dollars), inexpensive money management software like Quicken or Microsoft Money are great tools that can help you track your spending habits.

I recommend that you backtrack and input everything you can from the present year, although I realize that can be a pain, depending on what time of year you're reading this book. You need to gain an annual perspective, however.

Once you've input your paychecks, checkbook entries, credit card statements, utility, phone, cable TV bills, and taken a guess at your cash expenditures, are you in the black? If so, that means you've earned more money than you've spent. You are to be congratulated, saluted as a hero to the economy, and praised from on high.

Or are you bleeding red? Then you're like most Americans, spending a little more than you take in. The problem with spending a little more is that a trickle can turn into a torrent until you are hemorrhaging money, either from a small wound or a gaping hole that's gushing red ink. You need to determine in which categories you're doing well and in which areas you are overspending. You won't have any idea until you figure out what you can afford to spend for your level of income.

Mahlon Hetrick, a Christian financial counselor in Ft. Myers, Florida, once told me that people do not usually have a money problem. He said that people have an ignorance problem about money matters. I know that sounds rather blunt, but Mahlon said that people he's met with over the years have attitude problems about money—problems with wanting too much, trying to buy something that everyone else has, and spending too much on a vacation. The average family, he said, spends about 110 percent of their income. You can get away with spending 10 percent more than you take in one year, but if you allow those extra expenditures to continue for several years, you will be overwhelmed.

Listen, folks, families who are spending 110 percent of what they take in are not acting wisely—thinking clear and straight. Listen to what Proverbs 21:20 tells us: "The wise man saves for the future, but the foolish man spends whatever he gets." I don't know what it is, but too many folks just shrug their shoulders about spending more than they take in, figuring that's why credit cards were invented.

Getting out of debt involves making an attitude change. I know that many women view shopping as a recreational pursuit. I understand the rationale: shopping is a diversion, and some people enjoy the "hunt." I'm all for that, but the advent of credit cards has created a mindset where it really feels as if we're not paying for something with our own money.

Being a good shopper means that it's all about using your head and saying no for a change. Don't you teach your children what "no" means? Sure, you do. Parents of older children remember the battles they experienced when teaching their toddlers the meaning of this word.

"No, Caleb, don't stick that fork into the electrical outlet."

"No, Molly, don't step into the house with those muddy shoes."

"No, Luke, I don't want you to go outside without your jacket on."

And what did your kids do? They moaned and whined and didn't like being told that they shouldn't do something.

Hopefully, we've matured beyond the tantrum stage, but nonetheless, we're not listening to God's advice. The Book of Proverbs gives plenty of practical instruction on the use of money, although sometimes it's advice that we would rather not hear. Quite frankly, we feel more comfortable continuing our spending ways than learning how to use money more wisely. Proverbs reminds us to advance the cause of righteousness with money but not squander it (10:16); be careful about borrowing (22:7) and save for the future (21:20). The first ten verses of the second chapter of Proverbs remind us that those who listen to God's advice and obey his instructions will be given wisdom and good sense to make the right spending decisions every time.

You can listen to God or listen to the world (*You deserve a break today...*). It's your choice. God's answer will allow you to get out of debt, pay your bills on time, provide for a better future for your family, eliminate worry and frustration, and honor him with your giving back to his work.

Let me amplify on the last point. I could be wrong on this, but common sense tells me that when families are scrambling to keep the bills paid and running up bigger and bigger credit card bills, giving to the Lord's work is one of the first things to go. People stop writing checks to support their home church, missionaries to foreign countries, or Compassion International children. Worthy parachurch organizations like Focus on the Family and Campus Crusade for Christ must cut back deserving programs when checks don't arrive in the mail.

If you have stopped giving to your local church because you

think you can't afford to do so, I urge you to consider this story by author and speaker Steve Arterburn, cohost of the daily talk show "New Life Live" heard on Christian radio stations around the country.

In Steve's early years, he was quite financially irresponsible and deeply in debt. His father had taught him to tithe, but he hadn't taught Steve anything about properly managing his money or having some "margin" at the end of the month. So each time a paycheck arrived, Steve would write out a check for 10 percent to the church. He never dropped it onto the collection plate, however; otherwise Steve couldn't pay his bills. He says that he was so far underwater in debt that he needed an aqualung to reach the surface.

Each month Steve would write that check and keep it right there in the checkbook, absolutely sure that he would drop it in the collection just as soon as God provided a miracle. That never happened, so after a few weeks had passed, Steve would tear up that tithe check. He felt horrible each time that happened because he knew that he wouldn't be giving anything to the Lord's work that month.

Steve sincerely believed that the standard of giving was a 10 percent tithe, although he understood that many people believed that tithing was an Old Testament standard and that we were free to give what we wanted back to God. Whatever the amount, it just made sense to Steve that one-tenth was not too much to sacrifice since he believed God had given him everything he had. Thus, Steve knew what he wanted to give, but he had messed up his personal finances so badly that he felt prevented from ever achieving it.

Here's what Steve decided to do about it. He determined

that if he couldn't give 10 percent, he could afford at least 1 percent to support God's work. The next Sunday, Steve left behind a check for 1 percent at church, which turned out to be a liberating experience. He felt great. Now he was a giver.

Some might criticize a faith so puny that Steve felt he could give only 1 percent. Some might say that if his faith had been stronger he could have given 10 percent from the very beginning. But the reality was that Steve did not have the faith or the desire to turn in even one of those 10 percent checks, but he did when it came to writing out a check for 1 percent. Result? He wasn't there yet, but he was headed toward God's best. Next, he asked God to help him find a way to double his 1 percent tithe, and before long, Steve was writing checks out for 2 percent.

Steve's finances improved, and I don't mean that he started making more money. He just started spending his money more wisely. He said no to some dubious purchases. Before long, 2 percent became 4 percent as he continued to double his gifts to God. And it wasn't long before 4 percent became 8 percent, and then he reached his goal of giving 10 percent back to God.

What can we learn from Steve's story?

At a time when Steve's finances were in disarray, he committed to giving God a minimum amount. One percent may not seem like much, but it was to him at the time. When Steve was faithful in that small amount, God honored that effort—just as he honored the efforts of those in the parable of the ten talents.

If giving to your church has fallen by the wayside, prayerfully consider giving *something*. If it's $20 a month, so be it. You have to start somewhere.

Steve told me that he was not just committed to giving 1 percent the first time he dropped one of those checks into the offering plate. "No, I was committed to 1 percent for the rest of my life," he said. "Each new level became a lifetime commitment. I can't tell you what joy it has been to give back what has been given to me. These days, I love to give. I make money to give. I look forward to writing as big a check as possible whenever I can, but I don't think I would have ever gotten there if I had not started somewhere."

A New Chapter

For many of us, getting out of debt is going to take a lifetime commitment as well. Have you started by counting up what you owe? Are you going to track your expenses so you can figure out where all your money is going?

If so, you're making a great beginning. Now it's time to zero in on how all that spending gets made. The prime suspect is the credit card, a 20th-century invention and 21st-century curse.

TWO

The Credit Card Freeze

Let me state at the beginning that I have nothing against credit cards. In fact, I'm a big fan. Life would be pretty darn inconvenient without plastic. You can't make an airline reservation, reserve a rental car, or book a hotel without one. Credit cards open up the universe of mail-order shopping and purchases on the Internet. And I've pocketed a lot of air miles over the years.

For all the wonderful doors they open, however, credit cards can also take you places that you never expected to go, like Big Al's Loan Consolidators or the Law Offices of Shyster Whiplash (*where our motto is: "We can protect you from bankruptcy"*).

While many folks wonder how they could live without credit cards, the charge card phenomenon is only one generation old. America's first credit cards were issued forty years ago, but it took only ten to fifteen years before they became so popular that you couldn't leave home without one.

Somehow along the way, however, those behind the credit card juggernaut pulled a warm, soothing wool over our eyes. The power of today's modern media convinced Americans of the truth of the following statement:

See that number on your monthly credit card bill? That's the total balance you owe us, but you don't have to pay that amount.

You only have to send us a check for the minimum amount, which we've conveniently printed in a box right next to the total balance figure. As you can see, the minimum payment is a trifling amount.

I can't believe how many people think that a credit card shouldn't be paid in full each and every month! They cavalierly make minimum payments every thirty days as they continue spending away, heaping each additional purchase—some dutiful, some dubious—onto their mountain of debt. Every day they prove the construct of Christian financial counselor Ron Blue, who states that people have a tendency to spend 34 percent more when they reach for a credit card. Human nature being what it is, paying by cash or by personal check—and actually having to count out the money or handwrite the big numbers—acts as a governor on spending.

This makes sense to me, since one would not seem to be as psychologically restrained from spending when all it takes is a quick swipe of the credit card and a scribbled signature to complete a purchase.

Buy Now, Pay Later

As I mentioned in the Introduction, the average U.S. credit card debt tops $8,500 per household, according to the most recent statistics from CardWeb.com. Since American families have historically added 5 percent per year to that staggering amount, that figure will surely hurdle past the $10,000 barrier before we know it.

It's obvious that most people never consider the real cost of buying now and paying later. Nor do they contemplate what an old sage once said about buying stuff on credit: "Spending money you haven't earned is like using up years you haven't lived." A massive amount of credit card debt is like reliving *Groundhog Day:* you're paying repeatedly for books you've already read, dinners you've already eaten, and vacations you're already taken. Out-of-control credit card debt is stealing from your future to pay for the present, and that's a terrible way to go through life. Many people call it mortgaging your future.

Excuse my bluntness, but if you're still not seeing the light, then do the math—please. Who in their right mind would pay an extra 18 percent every time they made a purchase with a credit card? But that's exactly what you're doing. According to industry sources, the average credit card holder pays 18.3 percent annual interest, which in many societies is considered a usurious form of money lending. You may shift balances around to "low-cost" cards, but that's just a delaying tactic in the credit card war that will surely end in defeat, as I'll demonstrate later.

For the moment, let's examine a real-life example: your refrigerator dies, so you shop around town before running into Sears to pick out a new $2,000 chrome-plated Kenmore with an ice-and-water dispenser. You reach for your trusty Visa card because you have only $4,000 sitting in your savings account, and there's no way you're going to use half your savings to pay for a refrigerator today. When you add a $2,000 purchase to your credit card balance, that single charge will become $2,366 of added debt one year from now, based on 18.3 percent annual interest. (Actually, the amount will be a tad higher since interest is compounded.) If you don't pay off that $2,000 refrigerator in one year's time, it's going to cost hundreds of dollars more in interest with each passing year.

It's funny and somewhat sad that some folks will shop all around town to save $100 on a new refrigerator but never understand how that effort goes up in smoke when the new $2,000 charge is kneaded into the dough of their outstanding credit card balances.

There are other tricks that the credit card issuers employ in the hope that you are napping. Did you know that the moment you charge that $2,000 Sears refrigerator you start paying interest? You don't receive a grace period when you're carrying unpaid balances forward each month.

Did you know that if the $2,000 charge puts you over your credit limit, you'll be socked with an "overcharge" fee, usually around $29? Actually, some people do know this, which is why they open a Sears charge account, hoping to receive an interest-free month before Sears' high interest rates kick in, but that does nothing to address the overall problem.

Furthermore, did you know that cash advances will take as much as a 4 percent hit (or $40 for a $1,000 cash advance) when you receive money from an ATM machine? Were you aware that after you receive the cash advance you'll be *immediately* subjected to a higher interest rate—usually around 20 percent—on that amount? Another irritating charge is a $5 minimum for each cash advance, which is rather steep if you want only $50 or $100. Finally, the most grating surcharge is the $50 fee to *close* a credit card account.

I hope the porch light is coming on because those are the burdensome costs of credit, my friend. Since many more families do not pay their credit card statements in full every month compared to those who do (70 to 80 percent of American households do not pay their credit card bills in full each month), the verdict is inescapable: as a culture, Americans cannot handle credit cards. The evidence is reflected in the fact that the percentage of families who are more than thirty days past due topped 5 percent of all cardholders—a number that has been steadily rising since the U.S. recession started in March 2001.

Card issuers are also boosting "charge offs"—that's industry lingo for writing off card loans that are uncollectable. Charge offs have been steadily climbing in recent years and are zeroing in on 7 percent of all cardholders. In addition, a surge in deadbeats has prompted bankruptcy filings to rise in record numbers: between 1990 and 2000, the number of bankruptcy cases increased 95 percent, according to the American Bankers Association. If you think that filing for bankruptcy will save you, the U.S. Congress is expected to pass new federal laws making it harder to wipe away your bad debts.

The credit card business must be incredibly profitable to withstand a 7 percent deadbeat rate and what must be hundreds of millions of phony charges from stolen cards and stolen credit card numbers. The widespread fraud is why I check and recheck every single charge on my monthly statement, and so far, I've been fortunate: the only time that I can recently remember something out of the ordinary was when a Swiss restaurant charged us $28 for a lunch when we were holding a receipt for $22. We called the restaurant, and they gladly reversed $6 in charges.

This was a trifling amount compared to most stolen activity. My parents recently noticed that someone had charged $5,000 on their card in bets with an offshore gambling site on the Internet. The bogus charges were hastily dismissed, which means the credit card issuer swallowed the loss, but credit card companies shrug off fraudulent charges because Americans charge up more than $400 billion each year, from which credit card companies earn more than $50 billion in finance charges. That's a lot of cheese, to use some baseball slang. Besides, if credit card companies were serious about fraud, they would require the person's photo on the card (Note: Nicole and I have our pictures on our credit cards).

But, Mike, a photo ID won't help on mail-order or Internet purchases. You're right, but I'm happy to report that some steps are being taken to reduce fraud on that front. When I recently purchased a new Minolta Maxxum 5 camera via mail order, I was asked by the phone agent for the "three digits" printed on the back of my card where the signature area is.

"Oh, is this new?" I asked.

"Yes, it's a new security measure," replied the sales agent.

I glanced at the back of my credit card. Sure enough, the last four digits of my credit card number *plus* three new digits were printed in the signature area.

"I'm happy you asked me for it," I said as I dictated them over the phone. What the extra three digits mean is that if someone gets ahold of my credit card *number*, he cannot charge anything over the phone unless he provides that additional three-digit number as well.

The "Fasten Seat-Belt" Sign Is On

Okay, it's roll-up-our sleeves time—time to get serious about turning the nose of your credit card jet from an upward trajectory and toward a descent on the *terra firma* of debt-free living. Like a Boeing 757 beginning its descent one hundred miles from the airport, it's going to take a while to sink through the altitude of debt. (For purposes of this chapter, I will direct my advice toward those seeking to erase their credit card bills without utilizing consolidation or home equity loan strategies.)

The passenger jet analogy is a good one. You don't drop from 10,000 meters (or 39,000 feet) or shed $10,000 in debt very quickly. It happens incrementally over time, with two pilots—you and your spouse—at the controls, checking your instruments, gauging weather information, and not deviating from your flight plan, which has three salient points:

1. Determine how high off the ground you are. Just as there is less oxygen with each 1,000 feet of altitude, there is less financial oxygen with each $1,000 in credit card debt. I remember the time Nicole and I climbed 14,110-foot-high Pikes Peak overlooking Colorado Springs a few years ago. After six hours of hiking, Nicole developed dizzy spells at the 13,000-foot level. Nicole gulped Advil and rested after every minute of climbing to counteract the effects of high altitude. It was a long, tough haul for her to reach the summit because she could barely breathe.

Those sitting atop a mountain of high debt have an equally difficult time gasping for air. Even though it's difficult to face your financial obligations squarely, you must begin by tallying all your credit card debts. You start by looking at your monthly statement and committing to memory the figure underneath "Your Total Balance," the one that's much larger than "Minimum Amount Due."

Is it a scary number? Remember, anything over an aggregate number of $2,500 is cause for alarm. Credit card debt is a slippery slope—it doesn't take much credit card spending before your legs slip out from underneath you.

2. Take a credit card holiday. There are several great reasons to stop charging and start paying by cash or personal check. For openers, it's going to be easier to get your credit card balances paid off when you're not adding to the pile each month. With steady progress made each month, you're encouraged to keep chipping away.

Another enticement to stop using credit cards is the fact that you'll receive an 18 percent discount on every cash purchase because you will not be paying any charge card interest. Another thought worth keeping in mind is that suddenly paying with cash shocks the system and renews your appreciation for what things really cost.

As you embark on a credit card holiday, this would be a good time to take inventory of the cards in your purse or wallet. Most households have several credit and charge cards. This is no sin, of course, but having too much credit available has proven to be too great a temptation for many families.

Simplify life and scale back to one card, which you can use for emergencies. Have your spouse hide it in a safe place, or let the dog bury it in the backyard for safekeeping, but you're going to find life much simpler with one card in the house. As

I mentioned earlier, Nicole and I have enough trouble balancing one checkbook, and keeping track of the expenditures of one credit card tests my patience each month. I can't imagine juggling two, three, or five cards, so give yourself a break from the hassle. Of course, canceling a charge card does not cancel your indebtedness.

Any "vanity" cards like Neiman-Marcus or Nordstrom's charge cards must be closed out. The so-called bennies from a Shell Oil card (rebates on gas purchases) or a Home Depot card (an extra 10 percent for the first purchase) are not worth the plastic they are printed on. These benefits are no more than come-ons to get you to spend more at their business—the same reason a casino greeter hands you a roll of quarters the moment you stroll onto the gaming floor. Casino bosses love to hand out $10 in quarters—which you could pocket or use to pay for a stroll through the buffet line—because they've studied human nature. Ninety-seven out of one hundred people will make a beeline for the quarter slot machines, where that roll of quarters will be gone in five minutes. They know the hook is set when people reach into their pockets and play with their *own* money.

3. Start this month to pay off the lowest cards first. I love this strategy. Let's say that you have a Macy's card with $338 in "hangover" charges. Your Goodyear card has $649—the cost of mounting four new Michelin radials on your Suburban. And your Visa card has a honking $7,442 amount attached to your name. For the moment, you can allocate only $750 per month toward paying off these three bills.

In concert with a reduced spending plan, send each creditor

$250 a month. The minimum payment for the Visa charges is 2 percent, or around $148, so at least you'll receive credit for paying off some principal. Under this approach, the Macy's bill will be cleaned up in two months and the Goodyear card will take a month longer. With those victories boosting your confidence, you can turn your sights on wiping out that Visa balance.

Granted, this was a simple example. If your financial situation is clouded by multiple debts—car payments, installment payments on a new big-screen TV, and orthodontist bills, then you'll want to look into Mary Hunt's Rapid Debt Repayment Plan (RDRP).

I've known Mary, the founder of Cheapskate Monthly and an articulate spokesperson for getting out of debt, for nearly ten years, and this is the best do-it-yourself debt-repayment plan I've come across. Repayment plans can become terribly complicated and time-consuming. Mary says that unless you have a Harvard degree in finance, it's difficult to manually create your own RDRP. For just $18 for one year's access to her web site, you can create and continually access your own Rapid Debt Repayment Plan, which automatically sorts debts by order of payoff and creates a month-by-month payment chart that you can print out and check off as you make payments toward those debts. The RDRP will also tell you the month and year that you will be debt free, which gives you something to shoot for.

I urge you to demo Mary's Rapid Debt Repayment Plan at Mary's web site at cheapskatemonthly.com. Once you see how much extra interest you'll be paying over the next several years (the RDRP displays that as well), you'll be spurred to wipe out those credit card debts as soon as possible.

Another good idea is to send in your payment as soon as the bill arrives. Paying early reduces your average daily balance, interest compounding, and ultimately the total amount of finance charges you pay.

What You Can Do in the Meantime

What I just described is the classic three-step solution to getting out of credit card debt. The sad fact for many of us is that it's not that simple to make continual progress in this area. It takes time to repay our debts, just as it takes time for a passenger jet to make a gentle descent into runway 9R.

As you begin making the effort to pay down your outstanding balances, life goes on, which means that food, clothing, and shelter must be paid for, as well as the few extras that define your lifestyle. I've already made the speech about spending less and grabbing the reins of out-of-control spending, so I won't repeat it here. But as you work on rapid repayment of your credit card debts, keep these ideas in mind:

- **When you do spend, keep track of your charges.** You need to keep a running total of your purchases so that you know when to lighten up. If you're continuing to use a credit card for some purchases—but trying to "be good"—it's imperative to keep close tabs on your spending. Call your credit card company, punch in your credit card number, and a computerized voice will inform you about your present balance. You can also access that information via your credit card company's web site.

  I recommend inputting each purchase into Quicken (or any other money management software). If you don't have a computer or are PC-challenged, you can enter each credit card charge into your checkbook, but don't bring the amount over to the ledger area. Keep a separate running total in another column. Another way you can do it is to put all your credit card charges into an envelope and tabulate the total.

- **Don't play the roll-over game.** Many financial counselors recommend transferring all balances to your credit cards to the one with the lowest rate. That's okay to do once or twice, but psychologically this puts you in a frame of mind of trying to lower your interest payments instead of getting those credit card balances paid off. Besides, moving your credit balances around—like a pea in a mountebank shell game—is not looked upon fondly by those who track your credit rating. They know what you're up to.

  The lower rates ("Just 6.9 percent!") are called "teasers" because they never are as good as they sound. You have to read the tiny, tiny fine print at the bottom of the solicitations very carefully to find out that your interest rate shoots up to the standard 18 percent within six months or that your new rate becomes "prime + 11.9 percent" at a certain trigger time. Do you know what the prime rate is? I don't, and most people don't either.

  More often than not, you're worse off than if you had stayed with your original credit card company because the rate in six months could be higher than what you're paying now. The most effective strategy is a friendly phone call to your present credit card company informing them that a rival credit card is making this fantastic offer, but you don't want to leave. *Perhaps if you dropped my interest rate by a few points....*

You should receive an approval because credit card companies hate to lose customers; they make too much money off each one. This explains why credit card companies troll for new customers to "switch" their balances. Banner ads for credit cards pop up all over the Internet, and I've received my share of annoying telemarketing phone calls during dinner time. And the junk mail letters! I often receive nearly a dozen a week, and I'm sure you do, as well.

I throw them immediately in the trash in my first mail sort-through, but I've read that these credit card mailings have a 1 percent response rate, which means that one out of every hundred solicitations results in a credit card switch. That may not sound high, but in the direct-mail world, a 1 percent response rate is huge, which explains why several hundred pieces of this type of junk mail clog our mailboxes each year.

- **Don't justify spending more with your credit card just because you "get mileage."** What you're paying in interest wipes out any benefits from airline cards—the ones where you get a frequent flier mile for every dollar charged. These days, frequent flier miles rarely are worth more than a penny a mile.

  Let's do the math. Most of the airlines require 25,000 frequent flier miles to fly anywhere in the continental United States. That means you have to average $2,000 in credit card charges each month to earn enough miles in one year. That's not a problem for most families, if they charge nearly every purchase they can. (I know this from personal experience.)

So, let's say you successfully charge $25,000 in one year, but you have $8,000 in "hangover" balances that you weren't able to pay back. Eighteen percent interest on a revolving balance of $8,000 is $1,440.

I challenge you to pay $1,440 for any round-trip ticket these days. The airlines have been bleeding red ink since September 11, and it's not too difficult to find coast-to-coast round-trip tickets for $200. Spending to reap airline miles is a bad way to fly.

- **If you are trying not to use your credit card but are fearful about carrying large amounts of cash, then get a debit card.** Most banks also issue debits cards with Visa logos that automatically deduct the amount from your checking account instead of sending the charge to Visa. I have a debit card for places that don't accept my MasterCard, like a Costco warehouse club.

- **Don't give your kids "training wheels" credit cards.** You're going to see a big push for the new Visa Buxx card (pronounced "bucks," of course) targeted to teens and their parents. PocketCard, Cobaltcard, and M2 are the other teen cards on the market.

    The concept works like this: parents load money (via their own credit card or checking account) into a Visa Buxx card, which looks and works like any traditional magnetic stripe Visa card. Even the teen's name is embossed on the front.

Parents can load any amount they want, but once that money is spent, the card doesn't work. The Buxx is being touted as a way to help parents provide spending money for their teens and to teach them practical money management skills. The concept sounds great, but I fear it's just another way for the credit card companies to train impressionable youngsters on how to charge their purchases. Before they leave home, teens should learn to spend no more than what is in their wallets, not to hand over a magnetic card to be swiped.

The Visa Buxx card was invented to tap into the free-spending teenage demographic. No age group spends more on consumer goods: Teen Research Unlimited figures that each teen spends $5,000 a year, but that doesn't mean he or she needs a Buxx card.

Nor should college students have their own credit cards. I've listened to the balderdash about young adults needing to establish their own credit, but I've read too many horror stories about college students who got in way over their heads and graduated with overwhelming student loan and credit card debts. Spare your adult children that misery.

My daughter, Andrea, attends Azusa Pacific University, and uses an ATM machine for her cash needs and her checkbook to pay for larger purchases. I'm sure she's envious of classmates who have their own credit cards, but she's thankful she doesn't have to deal with the stresses of spending more than she has.

- **Ditch the status "platinum" cards.** Aren't we beyond American Express cards these days? I've received my share of American Express solicitation letters in the mail, and their cover letters drip with snob appeal. You don't need to spend a couple of hundred dollars just to impress the waitress or cashier when you hand over your American Express card. Besides, that's probably the twentieth "gold card" they've seen that day.

- **Think beyond one month.** The best piece of advice I can leave you is that it's far easier to get *into* debt than it is to get *out* of debt.

Roadmap

I will have more to say about how to get out of credit card debt and about consolidation loans and other extreme measures for getting out of debt in chapter nine. Until we get there, I want to share my best advice on how you get the most bang for your spending buck, how to strategically lower your expenses, cutting back on restaurants, taking vacations that make sense, why gambling is a bad bet, and the insurance solution.

THREE

Wheels Adjustment

I would love to buy Nicole a fire-engine-red Lincoln Navigator, a get-out-of-my-way SUV that commands respect and looks of envy as it plies the boulevards and thoroughfares near home. As for myself, I would prefer something more sporty yet elegant—a coral white BMW 7-series or Lexus ES 300 with leather interior, Blaupunkt sound, and GPS positioning so that I would never have to ask for directions again.

I can stop daydreaming now. Reality these days is a dead-tired eight-year-old Mercury Villager with 168,000 miles of errands, carpools, trips to the mall, and family memories on the odometer. And that's our *good* car: our second vehicle is a rusting 1986 Toyota Tercel hatchback station wagon that feels as if you're driving an oversized Coke can with a lawn mower engine under the hood. The underpowered Tercel, with 157,000 miles, is not allowed to go more than fifteen, twenty miles from home. That presents problems in our family, which has four drivers and two cars. You could say that we're learning to share.

Don't get me wrong: I'm not envious of our neighbors and friends who drive late-model SUVs and extended-cab trucks; I think it's great that they can afford those cars. Keeping them gassed up would nearly bankrupt us, but I'm fine with that.

Both of our well-used cars are paid for, and we're going to keep them until they die on the road someday or until the kids graduate from college, whichever comes first. The Villager and the Tercel really are our "keep the kids in college" cars, and if the trade-off is between a Christian education for Andrea and Patrick or driving a spiffy SUV, then there's nothing to debate.

In the discussion about finding real solutions for getting out of debt, I wonder how many people understand how much more it costs to drive late-model cars versus something decidedly less fancy. Yet the desire to drive nice wheels runs deep in our culture, and for many people, we are what we drive. I understand that mindset because I grew up in car-happy Southern California, where Porsche reigned atop the food chain.

Porsches were too rich for my blood, but I developed a mighty itch for BMWs during my teen years. The boxy coupes and sleek, expensive sedans bespoke status symbolic of its trademark advertising phrase—the "ultimate driving machine." When I was twenty-three years old and had moved back in with my parents following college, I wanted a BMW in the worst way. That summer, I worked hard and saved up enough money to purchase my first—and probably last—BMW.

She was a beauty that made my heart sing: a three-year-old 2002 coupe with a sunroof, CB radio (hey, this was the seventies!), and dual Weber carburetors. The salesman explained that this Beemer could do thirty-five miles per hour in first gear, fifty-five in second, and seventy-five in third. I didn't have the courage to ask about the fourth gear.

The slick salesman probably took one look at me—a kid in his twenties who thought the world was his oyster—and knew what buttons to push. His sales pitch noted that BMWs were in such high demand that they were *appreciating* in value. If I played my cards right, I would be buying an *investment,* not a depreciating asset like other cars.

By this time, the hook was set pretty deep in my mouth. I mumbled something about the price. He hemmed and hawed like all car salesmen do, but said he could "sharpen my pencil" and "let it go" for $600 less than the asking price. I put a few thousand down, and we worked out a car payment plan that seemed reasonable for my monthly income at that time.

Over the next twelve months, two things happened: I learned how costly it was to insure and maintain a high-strung German sports car, and I met the love of my life, Nicole. Shortly after asking Nicole to marry me, I knew this expensive toy had to go. It was time to unload my "investment."

Finding someone to take the BMW off my sweaty hands wasn't as easy as the salesman had promised. It took me several weeks before some Iranian students worked me over pretty good, and by the time I signed the pink slip, I had lost thousands on a car that I owned for just one year. A bit wiser, I turned around and purchased a '69 Dodge Polara for $350. This nineteen-foot boat was just the money-saving vessel we needed for our early years of marriage.

My BMW story illustrates three points:

1. Cars always cost more than you think.
2. You swallow your pride when you go "down" to a cheaper car.
3. Selling and purchasing cars involves time, research, and patience.

As we search for ways to cut expenses, the easiest thing for me to do would be to say, "Looking to get out of debt? Then sell that nice car in your driveway and drive a beater."

Life is not that simple. The cheapest car you'll ever drive may be the one you're driving right now, especially if it's more than four years old. It's the newer cars that are the monetary sinkholes—two tons of aluminum, plastic, and safety glass that provide convenient door-to-door transportation in style and air-conditioned comfort. There's a price to be paid for that style, however, which means that in the quest to trim household expenses, you must coldly study how much it really costs to drive a car.

It's been said that cars are the "second biggest purchase you'll ever make," and there's truth in that statement. The trouble is that the biggest purchase—a house—appreciates in value while cars, especially spanking-new ones beckoning from the gleaming showroom floor, start depreciating the minute they leave the dealer lot. In your desire to get out of debt, you may have to unload one or two of your prized beauties and purchase used cars five years old or older.

I know: it hurts to read that.

Add Up the Hard Costs
Before you make any drastic moves—since buying and selling cars involves loads of time—determine how much you're really paying for each car in your driveway. What you want to find out is a cost-per-mile figure. You begin by creating a report for the last twelve months that adds up all your car-related expenses. You could use Quicken for this task. You should record all the hard costs—car payments, insurance, gas fill-ups, oil changes, repairs, and new tires. The hidden costs, such as finance charges on a lease or bank loan plus depreciation, are more

difficult to ascertain. Most people conveniently forget that new cars depreciate by 40 percent in their first three years. Instead, they see a monthly lease payment of $249 and figure the only extra is gas. They fail to add in insurance, registration fees, the tax on the lease, and gobs of depreciation.

The American Automobile Association can help you calculate those hidden costs. If you are a AAA member, drop by a local office and ask for a AAA pamphlet called *Your Driving Costs*. (Much of this information can also be found at various AAA web sites.) While noting that the costs of owning and operating a car vary widely across the United States, the pamphlet presents an excellent snapshot of how much it costs to drive a vehicle for one mile.

The per-mile cost to drive a fairly ordinary new car—we're talking a Chevrolet Cavalier LS, a Ford Taurus SEL, or a Mercury Grand Marquis LS—is 52.3 cents per mile. Put another way, this means that it costs soccer moms $5.23 to carpool the kids to a nearby game (ten miles round-trip) or $15.69 to commute each *day* to work (figuring a half-hour commute of fifteen miles each way). A one-hundred-mile round-trip to a major league baseball game would cost $52, while fifty miles in errands would be half that amount—$26. At least you can be thankful that you're not driving a Mercedes, where it's estimated that the cost per mile is almost *double*—a little over $1 per mile. Those are close to taxi rates!

At fifty-two cents per mile, it costs you $650 a month (based on driving a car fifteen-thousand miles a year) to drive a new sedan, a figure that astounds most folks, especially since we are talking about run-of-the-mill four-doors. The more popular Jeep Cherokees and Chevy Suburbans and Dodge Ram trucks are probably around seventy-five cents per mile because they are more expensive, slurp more gas (ten to fifteen miles to the gallon city driving), and are more costly to insure because car thieves steal trendy cars.

According to AAA, the cost to drive a five-year-old used car is half the amount—twenty-seven cents per mile, although I have my doubts. When I totaled up everything we spent on our two old cars in 2001, I came up with a figure of 36 cents per mile—and we enjoyed a "good" year on the repair side!

Still, the principle is the same: driving an automobile that's five years old or older is going to free up hundreds of dollars each month that can be applied to your credit card debts. Depreciation costs are lower because older cars are worth much less, and the state and the insurance company discount annual registration and insurance fees, respectively. If the car is paid off, then you are saving on financing fees.

If you purchased or leased a new car in the last year or two, you have a tough decision to make. I understand that breaking a lease is costly since lease agreements are written in favor of the dealer. Perhaps you can turn the car back in at the dealer in exchange for something older gathering dust in the back of the lot. When you're scrambling to get out of debt, you have to think outside the box.

The target is finding a car that will lower the cost of every mile you drive—probably something five years old or older with seventy-five-thousand miles or so. Don't look too depressed. Dealers can do wonders with a used car make-over, taking out the door dings, replacing sanded windshields, shampooing the upholstery, and spritzing some diabolical exudates to replicate that intoxicating new car smell. If you have a nose for smell, call it *eau de saved money*. (If you happen to purchase an older car from a private party, auto detailers can perform the same restoration magic for $150.)

How should you pay for a new used car?

Hopefully, you are not "upside down" in your current wheels, which means you owe more than the car is worth. You will find that dealers are only too happy to re-lease cars that come back in, often at rates more favorable than a bank loan. If there is any way possible, though, I would try to put down as much cash as you can. You're better off buying a $5,000 used car for cash rather than putting down $5K and financing $5,000. The idea is to get rid of debt, not add more or just exchange one payment for another.

Kicking Tires

You definitely have to do your due diligence when buying used; otherwise you're buying someone else's problem. You should never buy a car without having it checked by a trusted mechanic, although it's a hassle to drive the car to his shop and pay $50 each time. Hassle yourself. The most powerful tool you have is the Carfax Vehicle History Report (carfax.com), which will give you a rather complete history of the auto. You enter the vehicle identification number (VIN), and up pops DMV records, previous leases, police reports, accidents, and inspection stations where odometer readings were taken. The cost is $19.99 for unlimited access and $14.99 to run one car through their data banks.

I'm afraid there is a real problem out there with wrecked cars being rebuilt and resold. These are severely damaged cars that have been "totaled" in an accident—often with fatalities—but instead of a one-way trip to the junkyard, the insurance companies make a few bucks selling the wrecks at auto auctions. It's amazing how these wrecks can be brought back to life, but they are, and unsuspecting customers are tooling around town in cars that were creamed in an accident.

Consumer Reports estimates that 3 percent of the thirteen million used vehicles sold in 2001 were rebuilt wrecks. For instance, thousands of cars were damaged in Lower Manhattan on 9/11, cars that were salvaged, rebuilt, and sold at auctions. Tropical Storm Allison flooded twenty-thousand Houston homes and cars in 2001, and thousands more have been flooded in Florida hurricanes in the recent past. Those cars are fixed up and shipped to auction houses, which means that a flood-damaged car could end up on a lot near you. Always run a car title history on Carfax.

When shopping for a used car, you have four avenues to choose from. Let's take a closer look at each one:

1. The dealer lots. You know the advertising jingle: *We take the best and wholesale the rest.* That's true to some extent, but you pay more to purchase a used car on a dealer lot, albeit you exit with more peace of mind. Many dealers can't take the chance of selling shoddy products since they have a reputation to protect. Some buyers believe that used cars are checked closely in the service bay before being allowed on the lot.

Dealers have lots of "product" to sell because of leasing, which came to the fore in the 1990s. With Detroit automakers subsidizing leases so they could keep their assembly plants humming ("Zero Percent Financing OAC"!), more and more leased cars are returning to the dealers after their twenty-four, thirty-six, or forty-eight-month leases are up. These leased cars come back with thirty-thousand to forty-five-thousand to sixty-thousand miles—models that can be resold or re-leased. When the cars are returned, the dealer supposedly inspects and reconditions each used car according to a factory checklist, replacing tires, belts, brakes, and torn upholstery. These refurbished cars are then "certified" for resale and backed by limited warranties from the factory.

These developments explain why dealers are now selling more used cars than new ones—a first-ever for the industry. Another reason why dealerships like to sell used cars is because you don't know what they paid for the car.

What a crazy business! Savvy shoppers for new cars can order printouts from Consumer Reports ($12 per vehicle at 800-657-7378) showing the "invoice" price (what the dealer is charged by the manufacturer) and the "sticker" price (what the dealer wants you to pay). Smart buyers negotiate from the invoice price up, rather than from the sticker price down.

That negotiation advantage is lost in the used car market, and to compensate, you'll have to do your homework by consulting the *Kelley Blue Book* as well as *Consumer Reports* and *Edmund's*. (You can find these resources online or at your local library.) Once you're confident that you know what certain models cost, it's time to visit some dealerships. Remember, you're on their territory now, and you'll run into a car salesman who does this every day for a living, so he is an expert at "controlling" the situation.

Play your cards close to the vest and explain your situation: you need to lower the cost of every mile you drive. Stay calm. You're the buyer, and there aren't *that* many people buying cars these days. Test-drive the car, testing the car for handling, engine power, and interior noise levels. It's not a bad idea to bring your spouse along to act as a "holdout"—someone who's not quite convinced that this is the deal to make.

When you sit down at the negotiating table, steel yourself for the tricks of the trade. You'll be put on the defensive by being asked whether you are a "today buyer," someone who's serious about getting the deal done. Be careful about making the first offer; wait to hear what he has to say first. Finally, be prepared to walk when negotiations bog down.

2. Private party. The upside to buying from a private party is that you should be able to save thousands of dollars. The downside is that you really don't know what you're buying.

Most people start with the local classifieds, but nearly every city has *Recycler* or *Auto Trader* tabloids found at convenience stores. Don't expect the grainy black-and-white photos to reveal much, but at least you get some idea of the car's shape. Once you've scoured the classifieds, read "How to Buy a Used Car and Avoid Scams" on carbuyingtips.com; there you can find questions you can ask the seller and learn about the pitfalls of buying from a private party.

You can gain the upper hand by doing your research onwhat the car is worth at market value. Often, there's a large disparity between what the car is actually worth "on the street" and the inflated value inside the seller's head. Ads from the *Auto Trader* for the same make and model can bolster your case.

Maybe you're like me—not the confrontational type. Maybe you don't enjoy haggling over the price. If you are armed with the facts, know what certain models cost, and have run the car's VIN number through carfax.com, you can rest assured that you are in the driver's seat when it comes to making a deal.

3. Mom-and-pop lots. Every city has them—the small, independent used car lots, where Rodney Dangerfield lookalikes hold sway over their dusty inventory. My guess is that you have to be on your toes since you're really buying these used cars "as is." I think it would be interesting to run a Carfax report on some of the cars that end up in these boneyards, but you never know. Be careful, shop well, and you might be very happy with what you drive away with.

4. Friends and family. They say you should never buy a used car from someone you know well, and I understand the rationale. A blown engine one week after a sale can blow a friendship, but the odds of that happening are not very high.

I like my chances when buying a car from friends or family: at least you're getting a fair scoop regarding the car's repair history. You're also more likely to be dealing with a Christian brother or sister, which again would raise my comfort level.

Final Thoughts

Let me close this chapter with a few more tips:

- **Don't drive an SUV.** I have nothing against sports utility vehicles; in fact, the coolest cars today are the Mercedes, BMW, and Lexus SUVs. The problem is that for the last five years, they have been the hottest products on the market. The automakers know it, the dealers know it, and the car-buying public knows it. With high demand, you pay more.

SUVs are Detroit's cash cows, making up half of all vehicle sales in the United States and two-thirds of the profits for the Big Three automakers. While the profit margin in small four-doors is rather thin, a Ford Excursion can pad the bottom line with $12,000 of profit. Besides being expensive to buy, SUVs are expensive to drive. You'll pay more for repairs, gasoline, and insurance.

If you need a hauler—and every family with children needs a seven-passenger car these days—buy a minivan. I know, they're not as sexy as SUVs and have suburbia written all over their front hoods, but minivans like the Dodge Grand Caravan or Chevrolet Venture will get you and the kids there in relative comfort, less style, and one-third less money.

- **Make that second car a beater truck.** Before we purchased our beater Toyota Tercel, I drove a fifteen-year-old Chevy S-10 pickup that was in great shape. Having a light truck as a second car sure came in handy when we needed to haul bikes to the bike shop, buy wood for the winter, or bring home a piece of used furniture found at a garage sale.

    I even referred to my white pickup as my "truck ministry." I let friends who were moving borrow the truck on weekends. I can remember the times when I had to borrow a truck from a friend, and being able to lend it out was my way to give back.

- **Don't get a car for teenage drivers.** Listen, if my teens survived high school without a car in Southern California, yours can as well. Your insurance rates skyrocket when there are more than two cars in the family.

Our most difficult financial moments came when Andrea turned sixteen. Remember, this was 1998, and we were in survival mode after I went all those months without a paycheck. We did not have the money to put Andrea on our insurance plan, so we asked her not to get her driver's license when she turned sixteen. In the meantime, we told Andrea that we would drive her everywhere—to friends' homes after school, to birthday parties on Saturday night, to the movies with her friends—and we would return to pick her up. It wasn't fun pulling myself off the couch at 11:30 on a Saturday night and driving a half hour to pick Andrea and her friends up at the bowling alley. But I did it, and I don't regret it.

There were a couple of unintended benefits to Andrea not getting her driver's license until she turned eighteen. We heard story after story of classmates crashing cars and getting into wrecks even though it wasn't their "fault." Not being able to drive at sixteen and seventeen freed her from that responsibility and kept her much safer.

The greatest thing about chauffeuring Andrea around, however, was that it turned out to be a great way to spend time with her and Patrick. Nicole says she wouldn't trade anything for all the mornings and afternoons she spent with Andrea and Patrick, driving them to school and back. More often than not, relationship-building discussions ensued in the "captive audience" atmosphere that only a car ride can provide.

FOUR

Get Thee to a Warehouse Club

I recently collaborated with tennis star Michael Chang in writing his autobiography, *Holding Serve*. For those with just a passing interest in tennis, Michael became the youngest male to win a Grand Slam tournament when he captured the 1989 French Open at the age of seventeen. The unlikely victory for the Chinese-American tennis prodigy made him famous overnight and led to a successful tennis career that reaped more than $18 million in prize money and tens of millions more in endorsements and appearance income. Michael may be worth millions and way out of my financial league, but he's a man after my own heart. Let me explain.

One evening, I was interviewing Michael over the phone. While I sat in front of my computer and tapped away, Michael answered my questions from his parents' home near Mission Viejo, a Southern California suburb. In the midst of our interview, Michael stopped me to ask an important question about a warehouse club.

"What time does Costco close?"

I glanced at my watch; it was just after 8:30 in the evening. "Our Costco closes at 8:30," I said.

"I think the one near my parents' home closes at 9:00," said Michael.

"Why do you ask?" I wondered.

"Because I have to go buy some tennis balls."

"You mean you buy your tennis balls at Costco?" I immediately had this mental image of Michael Chang pushing an oversized cart topped off with six boxes of Penn tennis balls through one of those cavernous, stack-it-to-the-ceiling warehouse clubs with shiny cement floors. I started laughing. The thought of Michael Chang buying tennis balls at Costco was like Julia Child dropping four twenty-five-pound bags of flour into her shopping basket or NASCAR driver Jeff Gordon purchasing a set of four radials off the rack.

"Yes, I buy my own tennis balls at Costco," said Michael. "I have to admit that I get a lot of funny looks from the young women checking me out."

That doesn't surprise me, but Michael shrugs off those funny looks because buying his tennis balls in bulk at Costco results in significant savings. I'm probably not telling you anything that you don't already know, but in this chapter, I want to explain *why* warehouse clubs are cheaper nine times out of ten on their unique product mix of groceries, appliances, clothes, and automotive items. But you have to keep your head; otherwise you might drop a $2,499 Sony Flat Panel television into your cart when you originally ran into Costco to pick up some milk and bread.

Go Grab a Cart

I'm not going to pass myself off as an expert on warehouse clubs, but I've been a huge fan of this shopping concept for a long time. Warehouse clubs were invented in 1976 by Sol Price, a San Diego entrepreneur who converted an old airplane hangar on Morena Boulevard (just a few miles from my childhood home of La Jolla) into a supersized warehouse that sold business equipment and various merchandise to "club members," mainly schoolteachers and people who worked at banks, hospitals, or local government offices—pillars of the community who weren't likely to write hot checks.

The kicker was an annual $25 membership fee that discouraged frivolous shoppers and added a little cachet: *ooh, you have to be a member to buy that fancy gas barbecue for $75 less than at Home Depot.* That $25 membership fee has risen over the years; these days, most family memberships cost $35 annually, but you don't have to be a schoolteacher or a government employee to be eligible. In fact, the joke is that if you're breathing, you qualify for a warehouse club membership, but most of the time, people get cards through friends. (If you're planning to visit your local warehouse club quite often, you might want to consider the $100 "preferred" memberships offered by Sam's Club and Costco, which include extra goodies like free towing service and a 2 percent "rewards" program.) Don't worry about wondering if the $35 membership fee is worth it. You'll save that much in the first "stock-up" visit, which will exact more than $200 from your checkbook.

Membership certainly has its privileges, and warehouse clubs provide entrée to a limited selection of quality national brands and private label merchandise with a wide range of product categories. Rapid turnover, high sales volume, and reduced operating costs enable warehouse clubs to operate at lower profit margins than discount chains and supermarkets. Generally speaking, warehouse clubs have a general mark-up of 8 to 12 percent, compared to 20 to 30 percent found at discount chains and supermarkets. From this small markup, warehouse clubs must make payroll and pay for their over- head costs. A Costco store manager told me the net profit is so negligible that without the annual membership fees, they couldn't stay in business. It can be honestly said that they sell their merchandise at cost and their profit comes from mem- bership fees, which approach 2 percent of sales or a little more than $1 million per store.

That business model is great for consumers, which is why there's always a little spring to my step when I flash my Costco membership card at the entrance. I know that the routine stuff on my shopping list—milk, Tropicana Pure Premium Grovestand orange juice, eggs, frozen strawberries, and frozen berries (for my morning smoothies)—are better deals here than at my local supermarket, but I also feel as if I'm on a bit of a treasure hunt. I like shopping the aisles in search of unex- pected gems: recently, I found ten Zip disks for $59, about half the price of CompUSA.

Overall, you can figure on saving 25 percent at warehouse clubs, although I've always felt I've pocketed more on specialty seasonal items that hit the sales floor, like Persian rugs or king palm trees. The savings can add up, especially on the large- ticket items. When our beloved Cuisinart died after twenty years of faithful service, we purchased a top-of-the-line Cuisinart for $189 at Costco. That same week, Nicole and I saw similarly equipped Cuisinarts for $249 to $279 in department stores and chain stores like Target.

Now, I know some of you may be thinking: isn't walking into a warehouse club a recipe for getting into *more* debt? Good point, because even a general "run-through" can nick your pocketbook for $200. It doesn't have to be that way, however. If you shop wisely and don't overbuy, you can save a couple of thousand dollars each year on high-quality merchandise and grocery items. So, whether you are a warehouse club veteran or wondering if you should take the plunge, here are some points to keep in mind:

- **Warehouse clubs have to make sense for you**. If you live in rural Nebraska and the closest Sam's Club is four hours away in Lincoln, you shouldn't be jumping into your family Suburban when you run low on milk and eggs. If you're empty-nesters or just a household of two, buying forty-eight rolls of toilet paper, six pounds of bologna, and a two-gallon pack of milk doesn't make much sense, especially if you don't have an appetite to eat bologna for two weeks straight or enough room to store a mountain of toilet paper under your bed.

  In their defense, warehouse clubs have gotten *much* smarter selling in smaller bulk sizes. It used to be that if you wanted to buy tomato sauce, you had to purchase a two-gallon tin—marked "Restaurant Serving"—and somehow freeze the rest. Now, warehouse clubs will shrink-wrap six smaller cans (each in a sixteen-ounce size) together for a single purchase. If you're making spaghetti sauce from scratch, then you only have to open one can.

  The problem with warehouse clubs is that many are not conveniently located. Warehouse clubs are usually situated on the outskirts of suburbia, where land is cheaper, or the only one in the city happens to be at the *other* end of town. If you are fortunate to live within reasonable driving distance of a warehouse club, however, then you're halfway home.

Basically, there are only three players in the warehouse club universe: Sam's Club, Costco, and BJ's Wholesale. I have never visited a BJ's, which are found up and down the Eastern Seaboard, since I've lived in California and Colorado all my life. I've belonged to both Sam's and Costco, and if given a choice, my pick is Costco. These stores have better products than Sam's, their return policies are the best in the business (if anything goes wrong or you don't like it, you can return it and get your money back), and they have the best free food samples.

Chances are, however, that you'll probably join Sam's Club since this Wal-Mart subsidiary has more stores in the United States than any of its competitors. Costco has a strong West Coast presence, where in California alone there are eighty-nine Costco clubs to choose from. BJ's are found from Maine to Miami.

- **Know your products, know your prices.** Warehouse clubs' philosophy of limited selection means they can't afford to stock losers. That means their buyers have to make the right call, and I'm amazed at how often they get it right.

  You might find only one brand of salami at Costco, but the Italian Dry Salame from Gallo is so good that it would make *mama mia* homesick for the Old Country. The fresh-squeezed orange juice from a local producer tastes like a delicious sample you'd find at a Florida orchard. The black leather jackets are sewed together from soft, high-quality hides. Even the fresh-cut flowers are good.

On items like television sets, stereos, computers, laptops, and other electronic goods, warehouse clubs offer low-end, mid-range, and bells-and-whistles versions. Our twenty-year-old TV recently died (it sure seems like a lot of our appliances and electronic items were relegated to the county landfill in the last year), and I was suddenly in the market for a new TV. I read a back issue of *Consumer Reports* to educate myself, and then I measured our entertainment unit holding the TV. The biggest screen we could get in there was a thirty-two-inch model.

So I went shopping—at Costco. Why go anywhere else? Costco had a Sharp for $379 as its low-end version, a Panasonic at $599 as its mid-range shopper, and a high-end Sony flat screen model for $1,999 that was not in the picture. So, the question for me was Panasonic or Sharp, and the display models looked and performed very similarly. My first inclination was to dismiss the Sharp, however, since I figured I would have this TV for ten, twenty years, and a couple of hundred bucks didn't seem much more to spend on an item that we would enjoy for a long time. But the more I thought about it, the more I realized that I need every $222 I can find (I have kids in college, remember), so I went with the Sharp television.

Good call. The Sharp is more than adequate for our needs. Fortunately for us, the Costco buyer had made the right decision on what "low-end" TV to bring onto the sales floor. Limited selection is the primary strength of wholesale clubs. Let's say you walk into Circuit City with their walls of televisions, all tuned to an NFL football game. Where do you begin to shop? How do you know that one television is better than another? Are you going to trust the sharkskin-suited salesman feeding off your commission to steer you in the right direction, or are you going to rely on the business acumen of the warehouse club buyer? In my case, I relied on the Costco buyer.

You see, warehouse clubs have a selling philosophy called "The Six Rights of Merchandising," and simply put, that means that they have to have the *right merchandise* at the *right time* in the *right place* and in the *right quantity* in the *right condition* at the *right price*. The right merchandise includes high-demand staples and commodities, sprinkled with a mix of new and exciting products. The reason you see great meat selections, superb fruit and vegetables, a well-stocked dairy section, a good selection of cereals, and a variety of foodstuffs is that grocery items increase the *frequency* of shopping. Every-one has to eat, and milk lasts only one week.

Outside of the grocery aisles, the philosophy of limited selection makes shopping easier and clearer for consumers because warehouse clubs often stock items recommended by *Consumer Reports*, although they can't advertise that fact. By focusing on limited selection, the warehouse club purchasing agents gain economies of scale all along the distribution pipeline.

- **Not everything is a better deal.** You can't walk around blindly and start pulling items off the shelves willy-nilly. If you know your prices, then you're aware that the boneless chicken breasts for $2.99 a pound at Costco can usually be found for $1.77 to $1.99 a pound at local supermarkets about once a month, which means it's a loss leader. Soda pop like Coke and Pepsi are usually cheaper at supermarkets for some reason. But nine times out of ten, as I said before, you're not going to go wrong buying an item at the warehouse club.

With regard to pricing, a Costco manager once told me that they have spotters and competition shoppers. "Let's say we have a Hoover vacuum for $179, but Target is selling it for $169," said the manager. "I would call our purchasing agent and ask him what we can do to lower our price. If he can't do anything about it, sometimes we'll pull the vacuum off the floor. We've even posted an announcement saying, 'Dear Customer: it is against Costco philosophy to sell at a loss. At the moment, Target is selling this item for less than our wholesale cost.' That surprises our customers."

Sometimes you find fantastic prices on off-the-wall goods like Versace handbags and trendy Swatches. What's the story behind them?

What happens is that the savvy wholesale club buyer will purchase goods "unconventionally" on the gray market. For example, Ashworth makes great golf apparel, but the company does not want to sell to a warehouse club because that would upset Golf Mart and Pro Golf Discount and the golf shops at private clubs. But let's say that one of those traditional retailers approaches the warehouse club with an overstocked item, or someone in the distribution chain wants to "divert" those goods to the warehouse club. Now you have something new and exciting on the floor again.

But what about fakes? You're right—Costco can't be selling counterfeit Seiko watches, or the company will lose a tremendous amount of good will. The merchandise must be authenticated to Costco's exacting demands.

- **Don't turn up your nose at private label items.** Costco started the private label revolution by selling its own club brand called Kirkland, and I've been pleasantly surprised over the years: Kirkland stuff is good! From dried fruit to laundry detergent, I've found the quality to be very high. I'm even starting to see clothing lines, such as socks and shorts, that are fashionable—and cheap.

  When done right, private labels can offer tremendous savings. The warehouse clubs like them because private brands cut out the middlemen with all their brokering and advertising costs, but it does make it tougher to comparison shop when the item is not available elsewhere. I haven't found that objection to be much of a problem, however.

  If you're a name-brand shopper—for instance, if you have to have Grape Nuts each morning—then you'll save between 40 and 70 percent buying the six-pound box of Post Grape Nuts at a warehouse club. That goes for other national brands as well.

- **Go ahead and go shopping when you're hungry.** A lot of frugal-type authors will counsel against going grocery shopping while you're hungry. While I agree with the tenor of the advice (that a famished shopper is so delirious with hunger that she absentmindedly fills her cart with Ding-Dongs and Haägen Daz), I think it's great fun and very "fulfilling" to shop at a warehouse club during the lunchtime hours when free taste treats are set out by those wonderful grandmas in hair nets.

  I will admit that our family has left church on a Sunday and made a beeline to Costco, where hot samples of creamy tortellini, chicken cordon bleu, and Chinese stirfry become our lunch. That's part of the "treasure hunt" mentality of warehouse clubs: you never know what mouth-watering samples will be available.

- **Generally speaking, you can't use your credit cards.** I should amend this statement to read: Generally speaking, you *shouldn't* use your credit cards because technically it *is* possible to go through the checkout line and flash a credit card. Sam's and Costco accept Discover (not my favorite credit card) or their own in-house credit cards. The credit door is wide open at BJ's: the store will accept MasterCard, Visa, Discover, and Nova.

  Even if you can use a credit card, resist the urge to use one, unless you are faithfully paying your balance in full each month and want the "rewards." A self-imposed credit-card ban can act as a governor on your spending, however. You'll be less likely to drop that Sony Flat Panel TV into your cart if you know that you will have to cover that check in the next twenty-four hours, and that's a good thing in this day and age.

- **Keep these thoughts in mind:**
  - Tires, especially high-quality Michelins and the private label Kirklands, will usually be the best deal in town, and the mounting costs are very reasonable.
  - Warehouse clubs have fantastic prices on eyewear.
  - Buying clothes are a hassle since you can't try them on at the warehouse clubs (except for jackets, of course), but if you're willing to take them home to try them on, you could be a big winner.
  - Salespersons are hard to find, but that's getting better, especially in the electronics area where TVs, stereos, DVD players, and digital camcorders are sold. I've had good luck talking to someone who knows his stuff at Costco.

A Final Thought

Whether you do the bulk of your grocery shopping at a warehouse club, supermarket, or farmer's market, you should stockpile meat and foodstuffs when they are on sale. By filling your pantry and freezer with good deals, you won't be at the mercy of whatever your local market is charging if you have a hankering for steak, for instance. It doesn't cost so much to keep stocked up.

Each week, the supermarkets put certain items on sale in their junk mail inserts and newspaper ads. The supermarket chains hope to draw customers eager to buy their "loss leaders"— and many of these items are sold at a loss—because history tells them that customers will fill their grocery carts with the rest of their weekly shopping. One week, boneless chicken breasts and corn on the cob might be on sale; another week it might be T-bone steaks and canned tomato sauce. If you know your prices and have the freezer and pantry space, then stock up and profit from your foresight.

FIVE

Why Take-Out Takes Your Money

I work out of my home, and one of the minor irritations is leaving my computer desk to answer the doorbell in the middle of the afternoon. More often than not, it's someone trying to sell me something.

The latest person to drop by was a well-dressed young man in his twenties with a restaurant logo on his polo shirt.

"Good afternoon," he began. "I'm with Papa John's Pizza, and we're here in your neighborhood today offering a fantastic promotion."

I tried not to look too interested, but he would not be deterred. For just twenty-five dollars, he said, I could purchase a great set of coupons. Two were good for two "absolutely free" large one-topping pizzas, while the remaining ten coupons could be applied toward "Buy One/Get One Free" specials. "It's a pretty good deal," he said earnestly. "We've been selling a lot of these promotion coupons in your neighborhood today."

"We never order take-out pizza," I said.

"Really?" The young man looked at me as though I were wearing a sixteen-inch pepperoni pizza atop my head.

I was serious. We never order take-out pizza, for several reasons: it's too expensive for what you get, it doesn't arrive piping hot, and the quality is uneven. When our kids were smaller, I liked to drive down to Little Caesar's and pick up pizza, but in recent years, Nicole has learned to make pizza dough in her bread machine. Once you eat Mama Nicole's homemade pizza— smothered with chunks of pepperoni, salami, baked chicken, black olives, artichoke hearts, and diced mushrooms—paying ten to fifteen bucks plus delivery tip for a single one-topping pizza seems like a rip-off. And the pizza never tastes as good or is as hot as Nicole's wonderful homemade variety.

I politely excused myself from the Papa John's door-to-door salesman, and I'm sure he hadn't encountered too many homes likes ours.

Now, I know what you're thinking: *But, Mike, take-out pizza is cheap and quick, and the kids love it.*

That's just my point. Take-out pizza is cheap, but only if you're comparing it to dining at Pizza Hut, for instance, or frequenting a Wolfgang Puck-type place that specializes in "designer pizza" topped with *canard à l'orange* and goat cheese. My point is that take-out pizza is not cheap when compared to the cost of homemade pizza. All you need is a bread machine ($59 at Costco) and the ability to measure some flour, water, and yeast and punch the "dough" button. *Ecco!* An hour or so later, you'll have malleable pizza dough. Slap some tomato or pizza sauce on, top off with your favorite ingredients and plenty of mozzarella cheese, and your family will be begging you for more at a fraction of the cost for take-out pizza.

My suggestion is that you and the family could tear into a juicy and tender filet mignon from the backyard barbecue for a lot less money than it would take to order take-out pizza or go out to Chili's. If the goal is to cut expenses from the family budget, then trimming restaurant meals, take-out food, and fast-food trips is the *fastest* way to save several hundred dollars each month—money that can be applied to your credit card debts.

Adding It Up

Do you know how much you and the family are spending in restaurants each month? On drive-thru trips to McDonald's and Taco Bell? If you're inputting your receipts into Quicken, then it would be a good idea to take a peek. If you're not tracking your eating-out expenses, however, then I can take a good guess for you. According to the National Restaurant Association, the average American eats food prepared in a commercial setting one out of every five meals, or 4.2 meals per week.

For a family of four, that means eating out seventeen times a week. If you figure that you spend an average of eight dollars per meal (I'm trying to balance the difference between fast-food meals and sit-down restaurants), that's $136 a week, or $544 a month.

I wonder if my estimation of eight dollars per meal is too low because it always costs more to eat out than you think. Let's say you invite the family to T.G.I. Friday's, one of the better chain restaurants that seem to be all over the country. You and the two children go easy, passing on the Sesame Jack Chicken Strips appetizer ($6.89) and the Jack Daniels' Steak & Shrimp ($17.99), which look too pricey. Instead, you and your spouse settle for two Blackened Chicken Alfredo meals at $10.29, which is more than you wanted to spend, but you justify the expense because the entrées come with house salads. As for the two growing kids, they're happy with cheeseburger meals for $6.79 each. Mentally, you're figuring around $35 dollars, plus tip.

But then you order two iced teas for the adults and sodas for the kids—bottomless drinks for $1.79 each. Although your waitress did her best to entice you with the dessert tray, you stood firm and ordered only one Brownie Obsession ($4.49) and four forks for everyone to share. Finally, you round off your evening with two coffees at $1.79 each.

So, what's this Friday's meal on a Wednesday evening going to cost you? When you add 6 percent sales tax and a 15 percent tip, the amount comes in at $60.20. But many folks think that eating at Friday's is cheap! Well, Friday's is cheap when you compare it to a tablecloth-and-candle type of restaurant, where the entrees start at $12.95 and zoom up to $22.95. The fact remains that it cost you $60 for the whole family to eat out at a fairly ordinary place in just one hour!

Okay, so you blew your budget by going to T.G.I. Friday's on a Wednesday evening. On Friday night, you're tired, you don't feel like cooking, so everyone piles into the minivan for a trip to Mickey D's—McDonalds. It's a lot cheaper to eat there, but it is still $15 for a couple of Chicken McGrill sandwiches, fries, and Happy Meals for the kids.

Finally, on Sunday after church, your best friends invite you to join them at Winnie's Diner, a family-style restaurant that's big on Formica tables and waitresses with big hair. Winnie's is cheaper than T.G.I. Friday's, but not by much. In this instance, "Sunday supper" costs $50 out the door. So, looking back at the week, you and your family ate twelve restaurant-type meals—less than the national average—but you still spent $125, which, if you did this every week over a month's time, would come out to $500.

That's too much money, especially if you're trying to get

out of debt. Listen, I'm no fuddy-duddy; I love to eat out as much as the next person. I look forward to the time of unhurried conversation, the period of family interaction, and the respite from the daily routine. It's nice to be served, enjoy excellent, mouth-watering food, and have someone else do the cleanup. The problem I have is that we pay dearly for the convenience, especially in restaurants that charge $60 for bland "mesquite" chicken breasts, nothing-special hamburgers, soggy fries, flat Cokes, and overpriced chocolate desserts in a deafening atmosphere in which you are expected to "turn over" your table in one hour.

If more families made it an "occasion" to eat out—like going to Winnie's Diner after church with some friends—instead of making impromptu midweek trips to T.G.I. Friday's, then significant savings could be realized. It's those midweek forays to Friday's, Chili's, and Applebee's that are killing you, so if you can eat at home a couple more times each week, you're going to save an easy $250 per month.

Dividing Up the Food Dollar

The National Restaurant Association says that we spend 45 percent of our food dollar in restaurants, compared to 25 percent back in 1955. Since one out of every five meals is in a restaurant-like setting, that means we're spending 45 percent of our food dollar on 20 percent of our meals. There's an unbalance here—and a place where some fat can be trimmed from your expenditures.

I could be taking another guess here, but one of the reasons you might be fighting credit card debt is because you've been "too tired" to cook or "too busy" to shop for food, so you've taken the easier route by eating out a great deal. I dare say it, but YOU CAN'T AFFORD to eat out as often as you have been. You're going to have to cut back and say no to some invitations.

The answer to eating out less is dining in more. I'm talking home-cooked meals because anytime you cook at home, you're saving money. And I mean *cooking*, not popping a frozen dinner into the microwave. Anytime you can do the chopping, dicing, carving, crushing, peeling, sawing, snipping, and splitting, you can pocket the labor savings—and also create delicious meals.

My fear is that we have lost the ability to chop and dice, to bake and broil. Not only is our culture losing the ability to cook, we are losing the desire, and that saddens me. I can still remember Andrea and Patrick returning from a sleepover and telling us what they were served for dinner—Kraft macaroni and cheese from a box, or warmed-up pizza left over from the night before, or even cold cereal.

I think there is a tremendous benefit—besides the financial aspect—to eating a hearty home-cooked meal with everyone around the table. The communal can-you-pass-the-corn talk prompts bigger discussions in which the family can talk about their day, about their hopes and dreams in the safety of those who love them. Lest you think that I'm as old-fashioned as a Norman Rockwell painting on a *Saturday Evening Post* magazine, I think that eating a "regular" dinner together is the best investment you can make in your family—financially *and* relationally.

Sure, it's difficult to get everyone together, with their soccer practices and Boy Scouts and Wednesday night youth group meetings. We adjusted by having a dinner hour that flexed with the kids' schedules. We've delayed many meals until 7:30 on weeknights so all of us could sit and sup together.

Finally, let me make this point. Each time you eat around the family dining table, you're saving anywhere from $10 to $60, when compared to the cost of eating out. Multiply that by two, three times a week, and you'll have some money to work with as you get those debts paid off. If you look at eating at home this way, this means your kitchen becomes a profit center—a place where you're *making* money each time you make breakfast, lunch, and dinner.

Quick Tips

Okay, I'm done preaching. Here are some strategies you can employ to stretch that food dollar when you're cooking at home:

- **Cook enough of the main dish to get two or three meals out of it.** Great-tasting meals are just as good three days later. Having leftovers in the fridge is the perfect answer to those evenings when you're too tired to cook or haven't shopped or are running out of time. Some leftovers taste even better the second time around. For instance, mixing leftover spaghetti noodles and spaghetti sauce in a big pan with some butter and heating it all up is absolutely delicious.

- **Have a freezer stash.** Some Saturday afternoon, brown up ten pounds of hamburger meat and then package it in one-pound freezer bags. Do the same with ten pounds of boneless chicken breasts. Then when you need a quick meal, pull a bag out of the freezer, heat it up in the microwave, and you have the fixings for a variety of quick meals—tacos, sloppy joes, hamburger casserole, chicken and pasta, and chicken quesadillas.

- **Use your Crock-Pot.** Every couple gets one as a wedding present. Don't let it gather dust. Throw some browned meat, vegetables, chicken broth, and water together in the morning, and you'll have a great meal that evening. The other added benefit is that by cooking up the ingredients in the morning, you won't be "too tired" to cook. Many moms, especially those employed outside the home, are too wiped out to cook at the end of the day. Doing the food preparation before you leave the house—while the kids are getting ready for school— could be one solution.

- **Buy a bread machine and a Cuisinart.** Bread machines are so ridiculously cheap—they've come down in price from $300 to $60—and so useful that every kitchen should have one. When you eat your own fresh bread, it's hard to go back to Wonder bread. As for Cuisinarts, these French slice-and-dice machines can turn thirty to forty-five minutes of food preparation time—time you don't have—into five minutes of food prep time. Once you get the hang of the Cuisinart, you'll wonder how you ever went through life without one.

- **Pack a lunch to work.** More people go out to lunch than for any other meal, according to the National Restaurant Association. When I worked in an office, I have to admit to a twinge of jealousy when my coworkers said to each other, "Where are we going to go?" A peanut-butter-and-jelly sandwich, some chips, and an apple were waiting for me in the company refrigerator, but I was saving $7, or nearly $150 a month. I told myself that I would rather spend that money on my family than on myself.

There was one other thing I noticed: it was hard for my coworkers to eat out in less than ninety minutes. That meant they had to work longer to make up for the long "lunch hour." As for me, I was out the door at 4:30, having put in my eight hours.

The same advice goes for the kids. Two or three dollars may not seem like much for a school cafeteria lunch, but multiply it by two or three kids and five days a week, and it adds up. You could even teach your children to make their own lunches, which gets them used to being around the kitchen, providing for themselves, and understanding that they don't have to be served every time they're hungry.

- **When eating out, watch the add-ons and drink water.** Appetizers and desserts can turn a $25 check for two into a $50 check quicker than you can say "shrimp cocktail" and "tiramisu." Eat desserts at home. As for water, having the family quaff natural liquids instead of Coke and Pepsi can save you about $8, when you include tax and tip. The bigger benefit is health-related, however, because water is much healthier than calorie-laden, heavily sugared drinks.

SIX

Setting Those Vacation Sights Just a Tad Lower

The following is a snippet of a screenplay about some good friends of yours:

EXTERIOR SHOT: BRIAN AND JENNA'S HOUSE

A father and mother are shown leaving the front door, where thousands of cheering parents have converged upon their house after hearing that Brian and Jenna have just paid off all their credit card debt. Amid the roaring crowd, a TV interviewer jams a microphone at the young couple.

Interviewer

Brian and Jenna, after years of effort, you no longer owe any credit card companies any more money. What are you going to do to celebrate?

Brian and Jenna

Why, we're going to Disney World!

No, Brian and Jenna, you're not going to celebrate your monumental achievement of getting out of debt by going back into *more* debt. There are plenty of ways to relax and have a good time with the kids that don't cost thousands of dollars.

I don't want to rain on anyone's Main Street Electrical Parade, but for those of you still weighed down by thousands of dollars of credit card expenditures, you shouldn't be going to Disney World this year either. A typical trip to Orlando runs around $500 *a day* for a family of four, when you factor in airfare, rental car, gas, food, lodging, park admissions, four T-shirts, and two sets of mouse ears. I don't see how you can do a five-day jaunt for less than $2,500 if you're flying into Orlando from, say, Omaha, Nebraska.

But, Mike, the kids deserve a trip to the Magic Kingdom. I understand, and my family has a soft place in our hearts for the "Happiest Place on Earth" as well. We live in Southern California, where Disneyland is less than two hours away by car, but even a day trip to the Magic Kingdom is an exercise in *cha-ching, cha-ching.* Disneyland clips you from the moment you drive into the parking garage ($7), pay the stratospheric admission fees ($43 a day if you're ten and older), wolf down fast food in Tomorrowland (I dare you to find a simple burger, fries, and a soft drink for less than $9), and buy a souvenir or snack (how about bottled water for $3?). A day of Disney will cost a family of four about $250 for meals, snacks, long lines—and some great memories. One of the great mysteries of life is how the passage of time weeds out the painful memories of long waits in line and preserves, instead, the memories of the exciting ride that followed.

That explains why many families draw the line against cutting the annual trip to Disneyland or Disney World or any number of regional amusement parks—they don't want to "deprive" the children. In the war against debt, expensive vacations are never the first casualty, although they often should be. My gut feeling is that too many parents can't bring themselves to say no to Mickey and yes to a cheap week at Uncle Bob's cabin at the lake. *Put it on the card and worry about it later* seems to be the prevailing attitude.

I must admit that I understand the thinking. Looking back, there have been some years when we probably couldn't afford some of our family vacations. We've made a few trips to Switzerland because my wife, Nicole, is Swiss, and all her family is still in the Old Country. We have saved and scrimped to fly over there because we want her parents to spend time with and get to know their grandchildren, and Nicole gets homesick for Swiss cheese and chocolate. Fortunately, our Swiss vacation expenses haven't cost much more than four round-trip tickets to Zurich since her parents feed and house us, but $2,800 for four summertime airfares financially stretched us each time we made the long trip.

Despite our tight finances, I'm glad we went ahead and took the Swiss trips every two or three years because the memories have been priceless. We didn't go into debt to make those trips, but we made up for them by vacationing on the cheap in the years we didn't go to Switzerland. We saved money by making day trips close to home or staying with friends when traveling out of town.

Traveling Times

It will be interesting to see how willing families are to board planes and travel great distances while the War on Terrorism is fought. Following September 11, you could have run a herd of Rocky Mountain elk down Disney World's Main Street and not inconvenienced, any visitors for the first few weeks.

People's memories are historically short, and my armchair guess is that leisure travel will bounce back as the economy comes out of the recession. With all the new security measures in place, however, families that fly will be doing so with less pleasure and more anxiety.

Whether the vacation industry returns to the good ol' days is secondary to our mission, which is paying off our credit card debts. No matter how deeply Disney World, cruise ships, or all-inclusive resorts discount their travel packages, you will have to plug your ears to their siren call. This is the time to travel cheap until your credit card debt is wiped out.

In my mind, vacationing on a small budget means staying with friends or family. Each time we've bunked with friends or stayed with family, I figure that we've saved a minimum of $150 a day since a mid-range motel costs $75 and eating in coffee shops is around $10 a head. Even fast-food joints cost three to five dollars for a "happy"-type meal. We've also saved money on the road by shopping for meals at supermarkets. They often have great delis, but even grabbing some bagels, donuts, yogurts, or fresh fruit for breakfast or turkey sandwiches and chips for lunch will cut your vacation food bill in half.

When staying in other people's homes, we try to be Best Guests Ever by lending a hand in the yard, respecting our hosts' privacy, buying groceries, cooking meals, helping with kitchen cleanup, and taking them out to dinner as a thank-you. And we've always reciprocated by opening up our homes to friends and family.

Our most recent family vacation was a driving trip up the

California coast in which we stayed with friends and relatives for several nights, but we also wanted to show the kids San Francisco, and we don't know anyone in the city. I think we dropped $350 a day, which included a stay at a Holiday Inn near Fisherman's Wharf and trying to eat without spending too much. That proved to be impossible in San Francisco, we decided, where purchasing four croissants and two bananas at a bakery cost us $13. Fortunately for us, staying with friends along the way saved us enough money to pay for two expensive days in San Francisco.

Being houseguests really isn't that bad. We know the old saying that guests and fish start stinking after three days, so we don't overstay our welcome. What happens though is that everyone has such a great time that our best vacation memories have been made with loved ones and people we enjoy hanging out with. We've also noticed that the kids have instant friends since we've usually stayed with families who have children about the same age as Andrea and Patrick.

Out in the Great Outdoors

Another cheap way to vacation is to camp. Now, my idea of roughing it is staying at Motel 6, and Nicole refers to camping as "sleeping in the dirt." Why give up microwave ovens and soft mattresses for eight-foot boats and outhouses that are too far away when you need one and too close when you don't? The answer for many of us is tradition and a desire that our children experience the same thing we did growing up.

Camping can also be a time for the family to reconnect amid nature's canopy without the distractions of television and Nintendo. Campfires stir memories, prompt small talk, and as the evening deepens and the embers glow more faintly, nudge us into bigger talk.

Although we haven't camped enough to officially call ourselves campers, we've done it enough times to know that camping is usually an accident waiting to happen. If the nylon tent doesn't balk at going up, then nobody can find the can opener to pry open the Dinty Moore beef stew. And the "facilities" always stink.

Families know that going in, and that doesn't stop them. State and national parks are usually the cheapest places to camp, but sites fill up quickly during the summer. Make your reservations early. In California, you have to reserve campsites at Yosemite National Park or along the beach six to twelve months in advance!

If camping is too primitive for you, consider Christian family camps or "conferences." Usually held in scenic retreat areas, these camps provide meals, plan family activities from morning till night, and offer various accommodations according to tastes and budget. The goal is to receive spiritual and physical replenishment in a relaxed, enjoyable environment. Families are given the flexibility to do what they want, when they want.

It's your nickel regarding accommodations. Some family camps have lush condominium-like suites with all the creature comforts, including daily maid service. Others cater to families willing to "rough it" in rustic cabins and community showers. The average cost for a family of four ranges from $700 to $1,500 a week, but that includes all meals and activities. Mom doesn't have to cook, you get to sleep in sheeted beds, and you don't have to share a toilet with others. Sounds pretty good to me.

Some of the better-known camps are Spring Hills Camps in

Michigan, Hume Lake and Forest Home in California, and Sandy Cove in Maryland. To receive a listing of different Christian camps, go to the Christian Camping International web site at www.gospelcom.net/cci, or you can write Christian Camping International at P.O. Box 62189, Colorado Springs, CO 80962-2189 and ask for the *CCI Membership Directory*. This resource costs $10.99. If your questions still aren't answered, then call 719-260-9400 for more information.

Over the Hill and Up the Dale
Let's say you have some great friends who've invited you and the family to come stay with them, or it's your turn to see your parents over the holidays. You know that it's not going to cost much out-of-pocket once you arrive there, so the major expense will be for transportation.

Do you fly or drive? If you can get there in a day, it's usually going to be cheaper to drive there, especially if you don't have to pay for a motel room along the way. However, do you remember back in chapter four where I talked about the cost-per-mile to drive? A one thousand-mile round-trip over the hill and up the dale to Grandma and Grandpa's place would cost around $600 in mileage and probably another $100 in grab-and-go food ($50 each way). You might be able to fly that distance for as little as $150 a ticket, which means that a family of four would be better off flying, especially if you don't have to rent a car once you're on the ground. You would also save two valuable days of vacation time.

For those traveling longer distances, it's almost always going to be cheaper by air, unless the vacation spot is a long way from a major airport. Usually, shopping for "high season" summer flights is as predictable as the New York Yankees advancing to the World Series. Every April and May, the airlines launch a fare war offering deep discounts for summer vacation travel. The airlines are saying that if you will advance us the money now on purchasing tickets for "can't change" dates way off in the future, then we'll offer you a very good discount. Those waiting to book in June or July are never offered such good rates.

With the airline industry in a total state of flux, I don't think we can rely on yesteryear's model. My prediction is that the airlines will be quick on the trigger to offer deep-discount fares during these recessionary times if they don't get the passenger loads they need. We will see more and more "instant" fare wars that last for a day or two—maybe even a few hours. While it always helps to plan way ahead, being ready to book on a moment's notice can greatly help your cause.

The volatile nature of airline pricing means that you have to be an informed consumer. Since airline travel is the biggest expense of a "friends and family" vacation, here are some points to keep in mind when flying the friendly skies:

- **The jury is still out on Internet fares.** With the rise of e-commerce, it was predicted that online discount travel agencies and online airlines' web sites were the wave of the future.

  That Brave New World hasn't quite happened, although the airlines are taking bigger steps to drive customers to their web sites, where, presumably, it costs them less to book flights and they don't have to pay commission fees to travel agents. Sites like Hotwire, Orbitz, Trip, Travelocity, Cheap Tickets, Expedia,

Cheap Seats, and Priceline also play a valuable role for those of us who are price-sensitive. When you're buying three or more tickets for a family vacation, saving $50 to $100 per ticket could mean the difference of whether you go on vacation or not. (For a great explanation of how to use different ticket sites to find low airfares, go to www.cheapticketlinks.com.)

Some of the web sites approach things differently. With Hotwire, you fill out your itinerary, and then you are given a price—and no other information. You aren't told what airline or what time you will travel. You have one hour to say yes to the proposed fare, and if you do (by punching in your credit card number), the tickets are sold. No refunds.

The mystery shopper scenario works a little differently with Priceline. You make a bid with your credit card, and if Priceline finds an airline willing to accept your low-ball offer, the tickets are sold. Again, you don't know the airline or what time you fly on the requested dates. I'll have more to say about Priceline later.

The other travel web sites are more conventional. You type in your itinerary, and you receive a screen showing different airlines, flight times, and comparison prices. The fares are usually okay, but nothing red-hot. I've found better prices by going directly to the airline web sites. Southwest Airlines and American Airlines have been particularly good, with American offering a 10 percent discount to those who book online. I've double-checked that statement by calling the airline directly and trying to book the same fare, and from what I can tell, it's trustworthy, although I recommend that you practice due diligence each time you purchase.

Travelocity has a great "Fare Watcher" feature that automatically tips you off by e-mail when there has been a fare reduction in a certain market. You can type in your nearest airport and your parents' city, for instance, and learn when the airlines have discounted that fare. If the price looks good enough to book, jump over to your favorite airline's web site—they could be matching or even beating it.

Travelocity's twin sibling is Expedia—the "Big Two" in the cyber world of online booking. Expedia has a feature called Price Matcher that is similar to Priceline's "name your own fare" service. Another feature called Fare Compare informs you about fares that other Expedia customers have paid to your destination.

Who knows what fares should cost these days? The airline industry has this Byzantine fare structure that results in the airlines posting more than one hundred thousand rate changes each day. This explains why it is impossible for you—or a travel agent—to know whether the price of a flight from Chicago to Dallas suddenly drops from $259 round-trip to $179 unless you're checking every hour. When airlines slash prices, they are practicing "seat management," in which computers set the prices based on anticipated demand. If sales are slow for a particular flight, the computer stimulates sales by tweaking the rates. That's why it's smart to constantly check for new fares.

- **Priceline.com is a special animal.** Have you ever stood around the baggage carousel, waiting for your bags to come out, and made small talk with fellow travelers? I have, and those who've flown with a Priceline ticket are often gleeful about telling you how little they paid for their tickets.

I say bully for them. As for myself, I've never been brave enough to book with Priceline. The web site says you might fly anytime from six in the morning until ten at night, but I've been told that this means no red-eyes, similar to the policy with Hotwire. If you're adventurous, not time-sensitive, and live near a small, underserved airport where fares aren't discounted, give Priceline a try.

- **Know the other downsides to booking online.** Let's say that you book a flight on Hotwire and learn that you and the family will be flying on United. But your flight is canceled upon arrival at the airport. (Sometimes the airlines flat-out cancel flights when not enough people have purchased tickets.) Normally, United puts you on the next available United flight, but perhaps that was the last United flight of the day.

  When this happens, United usually books you on an American flight, but with a Hotwire ticket, things can get sticky since airlines don't like to honor tickets purchased through online discount agencies. You can try calling Hotwire with your dilemma, but there is not a whole lot they can do.

  If you book directly with the airlines, you could be eligible to be covered under "Rule 240," which requires carriers to book you on another carrier when your airline has delayed or canceled your flight. There are exceptions for bad weather and other reasons, but saying "What about Rule 240?" at the airline's customer service area could net you a flight on a competitor's airline.

- **Be willing to fly during "off-peak" times.** You don't have to fly red-eyes to fly off-peak. Flights that are convenient for business travelers—who have traditionally paid the freight for the airlines—are early in the morning and late in the afternoon. Traveling before 7 A.M., at noontime, or after 8 P.M. can result in significant savings.

  There are "peak" and "off-peak" *days*. Don't expect the deal of the century when flying to Grandma's house on the busiest travel day of the year—the Wednesday before Thanksgiving. You might get a better price flying Tuesday night or first thing on Thanksgiving morning, traditionally a quiet day for the airlines. Take an extra vacation day and fly home the following Monday. Christmas Day and New Year's Day are also traditionally light travel days, which means that the airlines are willing to heavily discount their seats.

- **If you have to fly in the next day or two, check out Priceline, consolidators, and the web sites.** When a family member becomes very sick, or if a loved one suddenly dies, you often have to fly on a moment's notice. Priceline lets you bid on flights for tomorrow, and this would be an instance where I would accept the uncertainties of my routing or time of departure.

  Airlines have a history of sticking it to travelers who fly on short notice. Even so-called bereavement fares cost double what you'd pay with an advance purchase.

  One avenue to explore is using consolidators, or "bucket shops." These wholesale companies buy blocks of tickets from the airlines at a discount and resell them on the open market for whatever the traffic will bear. You can find consolidators listed in the travel section of your Sunday newspaper in the tiny one-square-inch ads littered across the back pages. Or you can type in "airline consolidators" in your web search engine and find dozens of companies willing to sell you a ticket on very short notice. Some of the reputable, well-established consolidators are Cheap Seats (800-451-7200), Air For Less (800-359-2727), and UniTravel (800-325-2222).

Careful, though. Some consolidators have been fly-by-night operators that have disappeared overnight with people's money, although that has historically been a very rare occurrence.

- **Don't buy your ticket based on the frequent flier miles you'll receive.** With a frequent flier mile rarely worth more than one cent these days, a cross-country round-trip (six thousand miles) isn't worth more than $60. Purchase by price, especially if your wife and children don't fly enough to take advantage of the frequent flier miles being put into their accounts.

- **If you have a favorite travel agent, by all means go ahead and use him or her.** Generally speaking, I'll research and book my own flights, but I've used travel agents on occasion and done very well by them. The good ones can make the SABRE reservation system spit out fares that you or I could never find. I feel sorry for hardworking travel agents because it's clear that the airlines are trying to figure out a way to drive customers to their web sites and 800-numbers so they don't have to pay commissions. Until travel agents become extinct, however, I think the savvy agents are a great resource. I've had travel agents—the good ones—tell me they don't mind if I call in each day. They know the game.

- **Support your local Southwest Airlines flights.** These days, it's the Southwest Airlines of the world that keep airfares down. Southwest has the lowest CASM—or lowest cost per available seat mile in the industry, which means the airline keeps its costs lower than its competitors and passes on those savings to the general public.

  Southwest is very picky about the airports it flies into, avoiding the major hubs like DFW and O'Hare. But flying Southwest keeps the American, Delta, and United Airlines of the world on their toes—and their prices low on the flights where they have to compete with Southwest.

- **Finally, volunteer to get bumped.** One of the best ways to fly for less is to volunteer to take a later flight when your flight is full. If your family doesn't absolutely, positively have to be there at a certain time, then offer to get bumped. You'll have to wait an hour or three, but your patience will be rewarded with vouchers—usually $200 to $300—toward the purchase of future flights.

  You have to be proactive to get bumped, however, which means you need to inform the gate agent early on that you and your family would be willing to get bumped. (Obviously, you should know whether you are willing to get off the last flight of the day to your destination, which would color your decision to volunteer.) A family of four could earn $800 in travel vouchers for taking another flight two or three hours later.

My best bumping story is the time Nicole and I agreed to get bumped on a short twenty-minute flight from Los Angeles to San Diego. For agreeing to wait one hour until the next commuter flight, we received $400 in vouchers from American Airlines. Nicole and Patrick used those vouchers to pay for one ticket to Switzerland in early 2002, so the cost of a ski week in the Swiss Alps was a little over $400.

All I can say is "Thank you, Lord."

SEVEN

Why Gambling Is a Bad Bet

You won't find this line item in any family budget. It's an expenditure that husbands would do anything to keep their wives from discovering. It's also an addictive form of behavior that will take you and your family to Bankruptcy Court faster than any other pastime.

I'm talking about gambling.

Although gambling is an equal-opportunity vice, I would be willing to bet that many more men gamble the family's rent money than women. Seriously, gambling is an insidious attraction that causes grown men to take leave of their senses. What else explains someone's compulsion to throw hard-earned money on a felt table in the faint hope of winning back that wager and something more?

I can still remember the last time I gambled, although it happened twenty-five years ago. I was living at Mammoth, a California ski resort three hours away from the bright lights of Reno, Nevada. Back in the 1970s, Nevada was the only state with legalized casino gambling, and an overnight jaunt to the "Biggest Little City" was just the antidote to Mammoth cabin fever. Reno advertised itself as a friendly, down-home place, the type of neighborly locale where, as one friend told me, they smile when they take your money.

I was fresh out of college, collecting a minimum wage of $3.35 an hour working at the Mammoth Mountain Ski Resort. As someone who had played his share of penny poker in the dorms, I was ready to test my luck at Reno's blackjack tables, which took a two-dollar minimum bet in those days. I can still recall my racing heart and the tingling excitement I felt as I fumbled for some folding money. I was going to walk away a winner!

In probably three minutes, I lost five hands and ten bucks. And then the most wonderful light in my head flashed on: *You mean to tell me that I worked three hours just to play five hands of blackjack—and lost it all?* I sure did, and that was the last time I played blackjack. I schlepped away from the horseshoe table that evening and never gambled again. I even stopped feeding the slot machines a stray quarter or two rumbling around in my pockets. What was the point of working hard to fritter my money away so quickly?

With the passage of years, I can't believe how providential that was to learn my lesson about gambling so early in life— and for so little money. I'm reminded how fortunate I am each time I drop by a convenience store on a Wednesday night, where I witness a long line of folks waiting patiently to buy lottery tickets.

I actually feel sorry for them. Many of these people are working-class wage earners, friends and neighbors who hope against hope that their winning numbers will be the entrée to untold riches. I wish I could walk up to each one and remind them that the odds of winning are so low—estimated at fourteen million to one—that they have a greater chance of being struck by lightning. Just once, I would like to gather them with fourteen million others in a huge stadium so they could see how miniscule their chances really are of winning a state-sponsored lottery jackpot. Finally, I would like to tell them that they are being played for suckers. Ten percent of all lottery players account for half of all lottery sales.

That makes me angry because the last statistic tells me the people who can least afford it are betting the most on their futures. (Have you noticed that rich people don't play the lottery?) There's a word to describe those who play the lottery and visit casinos and bet on sporting events: losers, and they're usually in hock up to their eyeballs.

Across the Fruited Plain

Everywhere I look, state-sponsored gambling has become as American as apple pie. My home state of California, like forty-one other states and the District of Columbia, has had a lottery for nearly twenty years. State governments across the fruited plain pitch Lotto and Powerball as if it's our civic duty to reach for our wallets and play their games of chance. Massachusetts residents have been very responsive: the Bay State sells more than $500 of lottery tickets for every man, woman, and child each year! Can you imagine what your family of four could do with an extra $2,000 every year?

For Massachusetts, the camel nudged its nose into the tent in 1972 with a fifty-cent ticket for the lottery and a weekly drawing, but it wasn't long before the ante had to be raised to keep gamblers interested in playing. Massachusetts kept adding scratch-off and keno games through the years; today, there are more than thirty-three different instant scratch-off games along with daily lottery drawings.

Let's be direct: the Commonwealth of Massachusetts and forty-seven other state governments (Utah and Hawaii are the only states that have outlawed lotteries or any form of gambling) are in the gambling business just as much as any Las Vegas casino owner, and they're trying to entice more gambling through the airwaves. "Everyone benefits from the lottery," claims a television spot in Virginia. An Illinois commercial urged residents to dip into their savings to buy Powerball tickets. During the holiday season, lotto tickets are pitched as the perfect stocking stuffers.

What a scam! Only half of every lottery dollar is paid out in winnings; the other half goes to administration fees or straight into state government coffers. If by some incredible chance you do win a decent-sized prize or a million-dollar jackpot, the state *and* federal governments tax your windfall, taking more than one-third of your winnings right off the top! Furthermore, jackpots are usually paid out in twenty-year increments, so inflation makes each year's payment worth less than that of a year before. Once you deposit what's left, you'll be sure to hear from long-lost "friends" and relatives looking for a handout.

That's not what the public sees, however. They see a beaming truck driver with a John Deere hat holding an oversized check placard with tons of zeros while the media asks him how he's going to spend his newfound riches. Just once I would like to see the media interview lottery winners from past years and ask whether they think their lives changed for the better. *Be careful of what you wish for.*

I have a better idea for those who insist on playing the lottery.

I would rather see them take a lighted match to several one-dollar bills on a cold day. At least they can warm their hands before watching their money go up in smoke!

Tentacles Reaching Everywhere

Gambling has exploded way beyond lottery and scratch-off games in the last ten years. Casino gambling has expanded into many more states, floating gaming parlors are back on the Mississippi River, and sports betting is commonplace. I read a special report in *Sports Illustrated* a couple of years ago about the "dirty little secret" on college campuses—rampant betting on football and basketball games that generates much of the energy you see in arenas and stadiums. Bookies are everywhere, and most of them are students.

Gambling has become so big that Americans visit casinos more often than they attend professional sporting events. Collectively, gamblers lose more than $60 billion, which unfortunately is just a statistic and doesn't even begin to describe the human cost. Dr. James Dobson, the founder of Focus on the Family, who served nineteen months on the National Gambling Impact Study Commission, said he received too many disheartening letters from families whose lives were shattered by gambling. One was from Bob and Robin Cook of Lakeside, Montana, who sent their middle son, Rann—a good kid who went to church and was an honor student—off to college with high hopes for the future.

Away from home for the first time, Rann discovered video keno machines, the type of quick-play game that can suck money out of pockets like an air hose attached to a cashier's cage. (Video keno and video poker are so addicting that they are known as the "crack cocaine" of gaming.) It didn't take long for young Rann to lose everything he owned. He pawned his possessions, forged checks on his parents' checking account, and stole family belongings to feed his gambling habit. To protect themselves *and* Rann, Bob and Robin made the gut-wrenching decision to turn in their son to authorities. I can't even begin to contemplate the heartbreak that Bob and Robin felt when their son was incarcerated in state prison.

You don't hear stories like Rann's often enough. Families are often ashamed at the behavior of prodigal sons, and husbands who gamble—and lose—feel as though they are leading double lives. My church pastor told me that I would be surprised at the number of people in our church who've come to him for counseling regarding gambling debts. Those who gamble develop a propensity for betting money they can't afford on games they cannot win. It drives them crazy, and I can see why. You can never catch up.

Please, don't allow any sort of gambling to have a toehold on your life. There are fifteen million compulsive gamblers in this country who wake up each morning wondering how they can make their next bet. I imagine that many don't want to live that way, but they're hooked by the adrenaline rush that gambling gives them.

You may think you have things under control—spending just a few dollars a week on Lotto tickets—but gambling is so addictive that you should adopt a zero-tolerance policy toward it. You're not going to get out of debt buying lottery tickets or playing craps or betting that your favorite pro football team is going to cover the spread on Sunday afternoon. You're going to lose your money and go into *more* debt.

You can reverse your field and still change things around. Suck in a deep breath and realize that it takes tiny steps each month toward paying down your debts. Not only will you be headed in the right direction, but you'll experience deep self-satisfaction knowing that you are paying back your debts through constant, consistent effort.

A Religious Perspective

After Roman soldiers nailed Jesus to a cross, "the soldiers threw dice to divide up his clothes among themselves," says Matthew 27:35 (TLB). "Then they sat around and watched him as he hung there" (27:36).

Timothy L. O'Brien, author of *Bad Bet: The Inside Story of the Glamour, Glitz, and Danger of America's Gambling Industry,* says that story from Matthew enshrines "exactly who holds the high and low ground in the perennial debates about the morality of gambling." Jesus obviously took the high ground as he paid the penalty for our sins on Calvary.

So is gambling a sin? Or just stupid?

You won't find any "Thou shalt nots" in the Bible regarding roulette or scratch-off games. Although the Bible does not speak directly to the subject, gambling does violate several major themes in Scripture:

- Gambling encourages greed (Luke 12:15; Hebrews 13:5; and 1 Timothy 6:10).
- Gambling encourages materialism and discontent (1 Timothy 6:9, Psalm 62:10).
- Gambling discourages honest labor (Proverbs 28:19; 13:11).
- Gambling encourages "get rich quick" thinking (Proverbs 28:20).

- Gambling encourages the reckless investment of God-given resources (Matthew 25:14-30).

The biblical principle of respecting honest labor and productive work disallows gambling. Seeking to get rich in a way that avoids respectable work violates scriptural truth.

Second, you're practically guaranteed that you will lose your money. A few years ago, everyone got excited when a Powerball jackpot reached $295 million, although it was reported that the odds of winning had risen to the stratospheric eighty-million-to-one range. That didn't stop a twenty-eight-year old Bronx waiter who shall go nameless from going to the bank and emptying his $3,000 savings account—the one with all the money he had saved up for trade school tuition—to play one $295 million Powerball game. Sure, this waiter had three thousand chances to win, but he just ended up joining the other 79,999,999 losers.

Maybe you think that the lottery is a sucker's play. Maybe you think you can improve your odds by playing casino games: slots, roulette, craps, or blackjack. Sooner or later, however, the "house" will accept your hard-earned money—sometimes with a Reno smile and sometimes without.

So please, do yourself a favor and stay away from gambling. God will honor your obedience, and you can sleep better at night knowing that you are spending your money on things with a more worthy return—such as providing for your family and paying off your stubborn debts.

New and Dangerous Territory
Five, six years ago, it wouldn't have been necessary to write this part of the chapter, but what you're about to read may save

you thousands of dollars. More importantly, it may save you from hurting yourself and your family.

The invention of the worldwide web and easy access to the Internet via a home computer means that you don't have to leave the comfort of your home to gamble or view pornography—two vices that cost a lot of money. Not long ago, you had to fly to Nevada to find a casino, or you had to drive to the seedy part of town to watch a dirty movie or buy glossy magazines depicting naked bodies performing sexual acts. That's no longer the case. Popular casino games—like video slots, poker, and keno—and every kind of pornography imaginable can be brought to your computer screen in the privacy of your office or bedroom.

Many sites allow browsers to gamble with "free" money or download dirty pictures without paying a cent. They figure that letting you try out their casino games or take a long peek will entice you to lay down some serious money—usually $19.95—to see some more action.

Internet gambling is technically illegal, but that hasn't stopped dozens of sites—many based offshore in the Caribbean—from offering instant access to gambling. Haven't you noticed all the "pop-up" banner ads and full-screen links to casino sites whenever you're surfing the Internet these days?

As for pornography, did you know that 60 percent of all web site visits are sexual in nature? Did you know that sex is the number-one searched-for topic on the Internet? For all their popularity, virtual companies such as amazon.com—the leader in e-commerce—aren't profitable yet. But tens of thousands of hard-core XXX-rated sites are raking in *mucho* bucks to the tune of $1 billion a year. The *Washington Post* has called the Internet the largest pornography store in the history of mankind.

Even a simple word search can get you into trouble. Let's say your daughter asks you for help finding information about the book *Little Women*. Instead of being directed to sites about the work of literature and author Louisa May Alcott, you'll be directed toward porn sites with pictures of short, naked women.

Even supposedly free online peep shows cost you money. The owners of Playgirl.com and several other adult sites agreed to refund $30 million to settle charges that they were billing visitors who were supposedly taking a free look. What Playgirl and the other sites did was ask visitors to type in their credit card numbers as proof that they were of legal age to view the X-rated material. These unsuspecting visitors later found their credit cards billed for recurring monthly charges of up to $90. The scam took advantage of the fact that many people were not willing to fight adult content charges on their credit card statements.

If porn is part of your life, can you talk to your pastor or a trusted friend? They can direct you to resources that can help you clean up your thought life and lead you to repentance. As an added bonus, you won't be spending money where you shouldn't, and you'll have more funds available to knock down your debts. (Commercial time: let me highly recommend a book I wrote with Steve Arterburn and Fred Stoeker. It's called *Every Man's Battle*, and it will help you win the battle of sexual temptation one victory at a time. More than a hundred thousand copies have been sold.)

In the meantime, you should take some proactive measures

to stop yourself from gambling online or leering at the computer. Here are some ideas:

1. Keep the computer in a public area. Place the computer in the family room or some other area that is out in the open. You'll be less prone to have a "bad" site on screen if you know that your spouse or children could drop by unexpectedly. Try to find other things to do when you're home alone, like going for a long walk with the dog. Out of sight, out of mind.

2. Install blocking software or subscribe to an Internet service provider (ISP) that screens out pornographic sites. Blocking software such as Cyber Patrol, Bess, Cybersitter, SurfWatch, and Net Nanny use teams of information specialists, parents, and teachers to assist in classifying content. Filtering solutions are not 100 percent foolproof, but they're a start in the right direction.

EIGHT

Insurance Against Debt

When a bloated Elvis Presley popped his final pill and died in a drug-induced stupor on August 16, 1977, at his Memphis home, Graceland, a cynical Hollywood agent made this crass observation about The King's unexpected death: "Good career move."

When it comes to getting out of debt, could one of your friends be just as caustic? In other words, in the event of your unlikely demise, would the life insurance settlement be the only way your family and loved ones finally get out of debt? *Good way to get your family out of debt, John....*

Life insurance shouldn't be looked upon as the last line of defense against debt, although I agree with the thinking that the last thing you want to have happen upon your death is leaving behind a string of debts with your surviving spouse and children. The last time I checked, credit card companies do not forgive your indebtedness just because you happen to pass away or die under tragic circumstances—such as cancer or an auto accident. Your estate must make good on your debts, which explains why credit card companies send tons of direct-mail solicitations offering life insurance to clean up your credit card bills in case you fall off a turnip truck. (These come-ons are rip-offs, as I will demonstrate later in this chapter.)

Simultaneously, one of the real solutions for getting out of debt should *not* include canceling your life insurance policy (or policies). Financial setbacks or overspending are not good reasons for getting chintzy with life insurance, although I do recommend dropping fancy insurance "products" like whole life, universal life, variable life, or permanent life and replacing them with a simple life insurance plan called "term life."

Are you confused about what all these mumbo-jumbo terms mean? If so, let's review the two major ways that most Americans insure themselves against death:

- **Term life insurance.** Term insurance, in case you're not familiar with the definition, is a voluntary arrangement between you and the insurance company based on whether you'll be alive at year's end. If you're still alive, the insurance company pockets the premium you paid. If you die, your beneficiary (usually your spouse) receives a rather sizable lump-sum payment to use to start rebuilding his or her life and care for the children.

  Now, it's not my desire to be sexist in any way here, but let's be realistic: term life insurance is mainly a guy thing. Since the husband is bringing home the bulk of the household income in probably 90 percent of intact, two-parent homes, it makes sense to insure *his* life and not hers. The truth is that if he dies, she will probably prefer raising the children and not having to work full-time outside the home.

  If *she* dies first, the surviving husband often keeps his job and makes child-care arrangements, such as having grandparents help out or leaving the children with a neighborhood mom who does day care. I could be wrong here, but experience has shown this to be true. (If you are a single parent, then by all means I implore you to purchase term life insurance so that your children can be cared for in the event of your death.)

- **"Whole life" types of insurance.** I don't like to invest in things I don't understand, and I certainly didn't understand what I was buying into when I agreed to purchase a whole life insurance product about fifteen years ago.

    For a mere forty-two dollars a month ("You'll never miss it," promised the agent), I received thirty thousand dollars of life insurance on myself and twenty thousand on my wife, Nicole. Part of my premiums were placed into an interest-bearing, "cash-value" account that I could tap into at a later date, perhaps when the kids entered college.

    For six years, my paycheck was clipped for twenty-one dollars every two weeks for a total of $504 annually. That entire time I never completely understood what whole life or universal life or variable life or permanent insurance products were all about, but I figured they had to be good for my family because it was at least *some* form of life insurance.

    The light came on when a middle-aged insurance agent attending the same church as I asked whether he could prepare a prospectus that plotted my insurance needs. I told him that I already had a whole life insurance plan, but he said that he thought he could present something better suited for my "growing" family. Since I was under no obligation, he said, why not take a look at what he could come up with for me? So I agreed to sit down with him.

The agent handed me the prospectus. "Your present insurance is not adequate," he began earnestly. "The insurance plan I'm offering will provide for your family in case you're no longer here."

You mean when I'm dead, I thought. I turned my attention back to the "prospectus," which was really a pitch for a new whole life insurance policy. My head swam from all the figures and projections and expected payouts, but there was one figure I understood: the cost to insure myself with this "new" insurance would increase my monthly premium from $21 to $300 a month, or close to $3,600 a year. I forget how much the death benefit was (now there's a funny phrase), but I think it was around $150,000.

I didn't have anywhere near an extra $300 a month to work with, so I declined, but that afternoon, I actually understood what whole life, variable life, or any other "piece of the rock" insurance was all about: my premiums were really an investment account with the insurance company, for which I received a death benefit and a return on my investment. When I studied the numbers in the folder, I was being guaranteed 4.5 percent on my money—as long as I paid in for seven years. If I opted out of the program before seven years, the "surrender value" would be negligible. (That's when I learned that the insurance agent's commission eats up most of the premiums in the first seven years.)

I reviewed my life insurance situation and decided

that I had been traveling down the wrong insurance road. I had heard the term-insurance gospel from many quarters: "Buy low-cost, term life insurance and productively invest the rest." I became a believer in term insurance, especially after I did the math.

Over six years, I had paid in $3,024 in monthly premiums, so when I informed Aetna of my decision to drop out of the program, my "surrender value" amounted to $1,800. Bottom line: I paid $1,224, or $204 a year, for two dinky life insurance policies that would barely pay for the funeral and a good wake. As you'll see later in the chapter, $200 a year can buy a lot of term-life insurance—$250,000 for a thirty-five-year-old.

I will be honest with you: it was hard to pull the plug on that Aetna whole life insurance plan. No one likes to admit they made a bad choice on such an important purchase, and it wasn't easy taking a big gulp and placing that cancellation phone call to Aetna. As I recall, a friendly voice attempted to talk me out of my decision. I held firm because I knew I was paying very much for very little life insurance and receiving a pittance for the "investment" part of my monthly deduction.

In your quest to stay out of debt, you may have to make a similar gut-wrenching decision to cancel a "whole life"-like insurance product that you have invested in for years. Like I did, run the numbers. Exactly what are you receiving for your money? Even if you've paid in for *years* like me, I'm confident that you're going to come out ahead when you jump off the whole life insurance treadmill. The biggest benefit in dropping a whole life insurance program today will be the addition of several hundred dollars a month that you can apply to your credit card and household debts. To me, that's a no-brainer.

Make a New Plan, Stan

Simply stated, term life insurance is the most cost-efficient way to provide for your family in the event of your death. It's easy to shop for—just type "term life insurance" into your search engine and you'll be presented with hundreds of options, or you can contact direct marketers like LifeQuotes (800-441-0072), InsuranceQuote (800-972-1104), SelectQuote (800-343-1985), Veritas (800-552-3553), and Quotesmith (800-556-9393).

Better yet, phone my life insurance agent—David Holmes of the David Holmes Agency (800-327-8963). I spotted his advertisements in *World*, a Christian newsmagazine, and I've been with David for about eight years. He sells life, medical, and disability insurance out of his office in Cross Plains, Texas, and I've yet to find cheaper rates for my term life insurance, which is a ten-year-level plan.

So, how much life insurance should you have? The recommended amount is eight times your annual income. If you are making $50,000 a year, then you should have $400,000 in life insurance. Here's another way to figure it: for every $1,000 a family needs to live each month, the widow or widower should have $100,000 of life insurance. Using this equation, if your family has monthly expenses of $4,000, then your spouse will need a $400,000 lump-sum payment from the life insurance company. In this way, your surviving spouse could live off the interest income, if he or she is able to receive a 10 to 12 percent return on the $400,000 lump-sum payment.

No one knows better than I that making 10 percent on your money these days is a tall order, especially in these times of 3 percent money market funds and 5 percent one-year certificates of deposit. Since making the right investments is beyond the scope of this book, you should meet with the most trusted financial counselor you know, or listen to one who comes highly recommended for offering intelligent investment advice with a proven track record.

I'm not one to pile on guilt here, but a Christian husband has a moral obligation to provide for his family in case he unexpectedly dies. Scripture is rather brutal on this topic. "If anyone does not provide for his relatives, and especially for his immediate family, he has denied the faith and is worse than an unbeliever," says 1 Timothy 5:8 (NIV). God gives us that warning through his Word because he doesn't want us to rely on anyone else, or, I suspect, have a church or charity further burdened with another desperate family situation just because the father did not have the foresight to go out and buy some life insurance. Besides, the odds are that the survivors don't have any significant savings to fall back on—otherwise, those credit card bills would be paid off, right?

I realize that there are federal and state government programs providing a "safety net" for widows and their families, and that the U.S. government pays out survivor benefits to families with children younger than eighteen years of age. The average monthly payment for a widow with two children is about $1,400 per month, an amount that certainly helps, but it's not a long-range solution to getting a struggling family back on its financial feet. Despite the creation of Social

Security, a husband cannot morally and reasonably expect the government—or the church—to provide more than a partial amount of the money needed to keep bodies and souls together.

Let me offer another point regarding untimely deaths. I can assure you that the several thousand workers, tourists, and New York City firemen who perished in the rubble of the World Trade Center left their homes on the morning of Tuesday, September 11, 2001, thinking that it was just another day in their lives. I would have felt the same way because we were living in a time of peace, at least here in the United States.

I wonder how many of the three thousand or so who died that day in Lower Manhattan were adequately insured. Yes, we saw this generous nation give more than *$500 million* for the families of the victims, and one can assume they will be adequately taken care of. But what about those of us who die tomorrow when a drunk driver careens head-on into our lane? Will there be a widow-and-children fund offered on our behalf?

Probably not, which is why you need to take care of the life insurance today. September 11 brought everyone's mortality back into focus, and life insurance agents said they noticed a significant jump in business in the months following the attacks. The average size of a life insurance policy also jumped.

You're in Good Hands

Term life insurance is the most popular type of life insurance, and it's very cheap these days since people are living longer, which means companies can collect premiums longer and pay fewer death benefits. A thirty-five-year-old nonsmoking male, in relatively good health, can purchase $400,000 of term life insurance for $157 per year on a ten-year-level plan. A half-million would cost just $170 per year.

Another reason term life is inexpensive is because it costs less than 10 percent of what whole life costs, which seals the deal in my mind. So, in order to find the best rates on term insurance:

- **You need to be in good health.** They have a phrase for it: you have to be "insurable" to purchase life insurance. To be insurable, you have to be healthy. Insurance companies won't stay in business very long, for instance, if they take on a new client who has terminal cancer. Insurance companies are also likely to look askance at those who smoke like chimneys, work on power transmission poles for a living, or operate a tour business in Afghanistan.

  To prove that you are in good health, you will have to submit to a blood test, which allows the insurance company medical staff to screen you for preexisting medical conditions such as diabetes, leukemia, and the HIV virus. If the life insurance company doesn't require one, that's a sure indicator that will you be paying higher rates.

- **Shop for a ten-year-level plan.** You can buy term life insurance for one year, ten years, or twenty years, but you must take a blood test each time you start a new policy. That's why annual renewable plans can be tricky, especially after age fifty. Go for the ten-year-level plan, which means the insurance company will sell you a certain amount of life insurance and guarantee the same rate over the life of the commitment—ten years. You pay more in the upfront years, but you make up for that in the back end, which results in a savings of 20 to 25 percent.

A ten-year plan also offers you the flexibility to opt out and start the ten-year clock running all over again in case prices drop—provided you can donate a couple of vials of healthy blood. Just make sure you don't opt out of your present term life insurance until you pass that blood test.

Let's take another hypothetical, but one that is grimmer. Let's say that at the end of your ten-year-level insurance plan, you're shopping for new insurance. A nurse practitioner drops by your home and retrieves a sample of your blood. The laboratory technician, God forbid, discovers that you have prostate cancer. Of course, the new insurance company will not accept you, but you still can stay with your present insurance company because you cannot be canceled, even at the end of your ten-year term! The insurance company will, however, jack up your annual premium (probably times two or three) since they have no idea how healthy you are. But at least you and your family will be covered as you battle the life-threatening cancer.

- **Know that direct-mail life insurance quotes aren't the cheapest.** The same goes for those late-night TV ads. The best rates are found through research—calling 800-numbers, scouring the Internet (check out AccuQuote.com or Quotesmith.com), and calling top agents like David

Holmes. Do some legwork, and you'll save hundreds of dollars.

Insurance You Don't Need

Getting out of debt means being careful about all your major purchases, and that includes other types of insurance. For instance, you've probably heard that you can't go through life without some form of disability insurance. On its face, disability insurance sounds great—who wouldn't want to be insured in case you lose an eye or become disabled following a car accident? But in my opinion, the rates are too high to replace 60 percent to 65 percent of your income. If you earn $40,000 a year, you'll have to pay 2 percent of your annual income to be covered, or $66 a month. That's a lot for a policy written with loopholes in favor of the insurance companies.

You probably receive monthly direct-mail letters from your mortgage company offering mortgage life insurance. The pitch goes like this: in the event of your death, the insurance pays off your mortgage, offering you "peace of mind." Actually, this is just another form of term life insurance for the amount of your mortgage, and it's probably not near the eight times annual income that you should be insured for. For instance, a policy that promises to pay off a hefty $250,000 mortgage costs more than $250 a year. You can buy the same amount of term life insurance for $115 on a ten-year-level plan!

Then there are those come-ons for credit card insurance that come in the mail, and they are especially targeted toward those with substantial credit card debt. The prosaic letters promise to pay off your credit card balances in the event of your untimely demise, but like mortgage insurance, these premiums are 50 to 100 percent higher than term life insurance premiums. They are mainly marketed to those who would have trouble qualifying for regular life insurance, since they don't require a blood test.

You can also disregard any solicitations for accidental death and "double indemnity" coverage. These policies are no better than shooting craps with the insurance company. What are the chances of dying in a car wreck, in a plane crash, or by smacking a tree while skiing? Very, very low. This fact is of little comfort to the bereaved families left behind, but it still does not diminish the truth that accidental death is still a rare occurrence in our modern society.

As for double indemnity coverage, this means that the insurance company will pay double the face value if you die accidentally. If you're the gambler type, then the insurance company wants $200 from you to place the bet.

When it comes to insurance, you'll never go wrong by keeping things simple. Seek out adequate term life insurance, skip the exotic and much more expensive whole life policies, and you'll sleep more soundly.

Isn't that what good life insurance is all about?

NINE

Some Real Solutions

Now we arrive at the point of the book where the rubber meets the road. I'm directing this chapter to those of you who feel like your credit card debt is weighing you down like a two-ton load riding on an Indian pachyderm. Perhaps you've lowered your expenses by shopping in bulk, trading in your late-model Acura for a ten-year-old Taurus, and relying on invites from friends and family for vacations. Despite taking these measures, you're still spending money as quickly as it comes in because that's how you've handled money ever since you started flipping burgers in high school. You've always had a hard time saying no to something you want. *If you can afford the payments, you can afford it, right?*

You're going to have to check that attitude at the door because you're slowly being crushed by your debts. If your savings account has been sucked dry, if you're taking cash advances from several credit cards to cover the minimum payments on all the cards, if you've received phone calls from nasty creditors demanding their money, or if you're wondering how you're going to cover the mortgage or rent next month, then you're hearing the roar of Bankruptcy Falls just around the bend.

You have only a few moments to reach the safety of the

shoreline. The way I see it, you have the following options if you *don't* own your home:

- You can discipline yourself by closing your credit card accounts with a new resolve to chip away at your mountain of debt.
- You can declare bankruptcy and have a black hole on your credit record for ten years.
- You can get credit counseling and ask to be put on a repayment plan.

If you own your home, you have several more options, provided you have more than 20 percent equity:

- You can refinance your home.
- You can take a second mortgage out.
- You can take out an equity line of credit.
- You can gather your debts into a bushel and shop for a "consolidation" loan.

Those of you with home mortgages, however, should *not* refinance your home, take out an equity line of credit, or roll all your debts into one consolidation loan, as tempting as those options may be. I know that refinancing looks attractive. For example, refinancing volumes surged following September 11 when average rates for thirty-year fixed-rate mortgages tumbled below 6.5 percent, prompting millions of families to pull cash out of their homesteads. Many of those who refinanced for larger mortgages, however, used the extra money to buy new cars or make home improvements and ignored their lingering credit card debt.

This shouldn't surprise anyone who's a student of human nature. According to a Federal Reserve study, during the last great refinancing boom in 1998, about half of the $60 billion taken out by homeowners was spent on home improvements, consumer purchases, and vacations—lavish, I presume. The other half was directed into savings accounts, investment vehicles, or repaying debts.

Sure, homeowners in many parts of the country have enjoyed significant appreciation in their homes the last few years, but please, you're asking for trouble if you persist in borrowing against the equity in your home, which in many ways is "paper" wealth. Are you certain that housing prices are going to continue rising in the next few years? Don't be so sure. "Boom and bust" fluctuations in real estate prices are as old as the republic.

Today, when people look at housing, all they see is heady appreciation, however. National home prices rose 5.5 percent in 1998, 5.6 percent in 1999, and 8.4 percent in 2000, according to Fannie Mae data. Home prices were set to take another big leap in 2001 until September 11, however, which allows me to sound a cautionary note: when housing prices rise nearly 25 percent in less than four years, that rate cannot be sustained because it is beyond the rate of inflation and beyond the growth in family income. People's ability to pay so much for housing will reach an untenable point.

My feeling, based on my research and interviews, is that employing some form of home refinancing to pay off debts is like putting a Band-Aid on top of a bullet wound. Refinancing is rarely the answer because it's expensive: the small-print contracts are replete with hidden fees and costs. Refinancing can also give your creditors a better opportunity to seize your most important asset—your home—because you are trading unsecured debt for secured debt. As an example, you wouldn't turn your car loan into a second mortgage unless you'd rather lose your home than your car. The same thinking goes for consumer items purchased with credit cards. It's far better for the bank to repossess your "stuff" than take your house.

Experts say that those who refinance and wipe out their credit card debts often end up head over heels in debt three to five years later, in just as much debt as before they got into trouble. The problem is not having enough money on your hands—it's overspending. If you don't get out of the habit of spending 10 percent more than you make before you refinance, you sure aren't going to get out of the habit *after* you refinance. If you rely on refinancing to bail you out the second time around, you won't have any equity to work with, and that's when things get *really* serious.

People never think that such a catastrophic event—losing their home—could happen to them, but if you don't pay your mortgage, or your second mortgages, or your equity line of credit on time, your creditor will foreclose on you and take your property in the time proscribed by the contract you signed—a time that varies in different states, from ninety days to a couple of years. If you can't pay your credit cards, however, the credit card companies can't get your house. That's because credit cards are unsecured loans and not tied to any of your assets. Unsecured loans also charge 300 percent more interest than real-estate loans (the difference between 6 percent and 18 percent interest) since there is the risk that the creditor might go BK—bankrupt.

Bankruptcy is to be avoided if possible since many Christians feel that it is unbiblical to walk away from your debts. From a secular standpoint, bankruptcy is a black mark that stains your credit rating for up to ten years. You can forget about purchasing a home or a new car, and any other credit applications (such as a credit card) will likely be turned down.

No matter how bad your debts, or whether you let a credit card or two "slip away" as the economy headed south, there is hope to get everything paid back and start fresh again. Let me tell you about the best way to get out from underneath your credit card debt.

A Crash Course

I'm sitting in the office of Jerry McTaggert, president of Christian Credit Counselors, and I'm receiving a crash course in the world of credit counseling. The national office for this nonprofit organization is located in Carlsbad, California, about fifteen minutes from my home.

From what I can see, it looks like quite an operation. Around fifty busy employees handle calls, provide counseling, set up payment schedules, and send out necessary follow-up materials.

"Unfortunately, business is booming," says Jerry. "The latest recession has had a profound effect on our business. People have lost 20 and 30 percent of their incomes in wages and tips, and they are struggling to keep their heads above water."

"How much is business booming?" I ask.

"We have twenty-five thousand clients, and most are families where the parents are thirty-five years of age with 2.5 kids. Their average debt is $17,000 spread across five or six credit cards."

The number of clients—twenty-five thousand—astounds me. "How much do they have in savings?" I ask.

"Zero," says Jerry.

"How did they get into trouble?"

"They spend 10 percent more than they make."

Where have I heard that before? I think.

Jerry continues describing his average client. "Most earn around $40,000 a year, but they spend $44,000," he says. "You wouldn't believe the number of people who make $40,000 who say to me, 'Oh, if I only made $50,000, all my troubles would be over.' Then you wouldn't believe the number of people who make $50,000 a year who say to me, 'Oh, if I only made $60,000 a year. We would have it made.' They really do believe that. What gets them into trouble is that they make their wants their needs.

"I don't think any of them bought on credit not planning to pay back what they owe, but they always projected that things would get better or that a certain raise would come through. It's like the old saying: they didn't know they were one heartbeat away from death and one day away from unemployment."

"So what does Christian Credit Counselors do?"

And this is what I find out.

Let's say that you're a thirty-five-year-old father of 2.5 kids, and for whatever reason, you've run up a fairly typical $17,000 on eight credit and charge cards. Your savings accounts have evaporated. You've stopped making minimum payments because there's only enough money on hand to keep the mortgage, utilities, and food bills paid.

You see an advertisement for Christian Credit Counselors

in *New Man* or *Charisma* magazine. You call the 800-number and lay out your tale of woe. What happens next?

Christian Credit Counselors, using a sophisticated software program, prepares a budget analysis. The counselor asks for your monthly income after taxes and then a detailed description of your monthly expenses. Since CCC is a Christian company, the number-one item listed for monthly expenses is the tithe. Jerry said that many CCC clients choose to give at least something back to the Lord—$50 to $100 a month—as they crawl out of debt.

Next come the usual household budget items: housing costs, utilities, food, automobiles, clothing, medical, child care, and miscellaneous. You take the total net income and deduct the monthly living expenses, and you have a number that's available for debt retirement.

Jerry showed me a fairly typical client. Let's call them Jess and Jennie Thompson. Here was their breakdown:

Thompsons' monthly gross income after taxes
His salary:	$3,400
Her salary:	$1,400
Total net income:	$4,800

Thompson's monthly expenses
Tithe	$100
Mortgage and property taxes:	$1,550
Utilities (electricity, natural gas, water/sewer, trash, phone, and cable TV):	$500
Food	$1,000
Automobiles (car payments)	$560

Clothing (for children only) $70

Miscellaneous...$150

Piano lessons for children $130

Monthly living expenses $4,060

Total available for debt retirement: $740

That's the amount that the Thompsons had to work with after they made a no-frills budget with the CCC counselor.

Now let's turn our attention to their debts, which are rather dirty:

Creditor's Name	Principal Balance	Monthly Payment	Current Interest Rate	CCC Lower Interest Rate	Adjusted Payment
Bank First Action Credit Card	$668	$21	21.42%	0.00%	$21
Bank First Action Credit Card	$1,030	$31	20.42%	0.00%	$31
Capitol One Credit Card	$545	$16	19.20%	15.90%	$20
Capitol One Credit Card	$1,799	$53	17.71%	15.90%	$36
Direct Merchants Credit Card	$12,532	$316	21.24%	15.90%	$251
HRS Charge Card	$1,029	$30	21.95	9.0%	$21
JC Penney Charge Card	$1,741	$87	24.99%	15.84%	$44
Nordstrom Charge Card	$1,737	$90	21.75%	0.00%	$35
Providian Credit Card	$977	$29	23.99%	19.99%	$30
Providian Credit Card	$7,421	$223	23.99%	19.99%	$149

Creditor Name	Principal Balance	Monthly Payment	Current Interest Rate	CCC Lower Interest Rate	Adjusted Payment
Robinson May Charge Card	$313	$50	21.60%	8.0%	$20
Robinson May Charge Card	$341	$60	21.60%	8.0%	$20
Shell Gas Card	$763	$23	20.99%	12.99%	$20
Monthly Donation to CCC		$20			$20
Total Debt	$30,896				
Monthly Payment Before Minimun		$1,049			
Average Interest Rates			21.99%	13.55%	
Adjusted Payment to CCC to Pay Off Creditor					$718

Check a few things out here. It's obvious that the Thompsons were applying for new cards so they could get cash advances, which they applied as minimum payments to their card deck of credit cards. Their cash advances were hit with a higher rate, which explains why so many credit cards had interest rates in the low twenties. Can you believe how high their interest rates are? Maybe you didn't believe me when I said in chapter two that the average credit card interest rate was 18.3 percent.

Notice, too, that CCC was able to negotiate down several interest rates. Three creditors—two Bank First cards and Nordstrom—knocked their interest all the way down to zero. That's like their saying, *We don't need the interest. Just pay us our money back!*

Now you have a roadmap explaining what credit counseling companies like CCC do. Each month, the Thompsons have $718 automatically deducted from their paychecks and electronically deposited into CCC's bank account. (It's not that CCC doesn't trust the couple, but the Thompsons can't spend money that they can't put their hands on.)

CCC accepts that $718, from which they disburse the designated payments in the column to the far right called Adjusted Payment. Under this payment plan, the Thompsons' debts will be paid in five years and one month instead of *forty-six* years.

CCC is not a loan company; it provides a debt repayment plan—a structure to pay back consumer debts. The company negotiates with creditors of unsecured debts (credit cards, store cards) to get the lowest monthly payments and lowest interest rates possible, and consolidates all those debts into one monthly payment, which it then disburses to the creditors.

As with all clients, CCC insisted that the Thompsons call each credit card issuer and notify them that they were closing their accounts. Then the couple was instructed to cut up their cards, a symbolic but highly powerful act. Calling the credit card companies also helped the Thompsons protect their credit rating because their credit report will look better if they cancel instead of a third party like CCC.

Without the credit card crutch, Jess and Jennie will have to pay all their bills and make all their purchases with cash or personal check. The Thompsons will think twice about each purchase and learn to live on the money they have in their pockets and in their checkbook ledger.

You might have noticed that the Thompsons actually make very good money. I figure that take-home pay of $4,800 means a gross household income of $7,000 per month before taxes, or $84,000 annually. Many families reading this book would love to have $4,800 a month to work with, but the Thompsons proved that they were no different from other folks who spend 10 percent more than they earn.

You may also be wondering what CCC gets out of this. Their service is free to the Thompsons, although clients are asked to make a voluntary donation each month to the non profit organization. In this case, the Thompsons chose to make a $20 a month donation to CCC. Where CCC makes its money is from the creditors, who are only too happy to know that they are not going to have to "charge off" the Thompson debts. The creditors pay CCC between five and ten cents on the dollar, meaning that for every dollar CCC disburses to them, CCC receives a five to ten cent commission.

Christian Credit Counselors is one of seven hundred or so credit counseling firms across the country. The industry has gone through a period of consolidation in recent years because credit card companies have reduced their commissions from fifteen cents on the dollar to roughly half that amount. It's similar to how airlines have cut commissions to travel agents.

I highly recommend Christian Credit Counselors if you have reached a point where your credit card debts are overwhelming you. You can contact them at 888-520-4422 or go online at christianccc.org.

CCC is one of the handful of Christian-based credit counseling organizations. Others worth looking into are:

- **Christian Financial Ministries.** You know this is a good organization since it was founded by Larry Burkett, a

Christian financial counselor and author whom I've respected for years. Christian Financial Ministries has two debt reductions plans called Sure-Pay and Excel-Pay. The programs are similar to Christian Credit Counselors except that Christian Financial Ministries asks you to go through a Bible study workbook and a budgeting work-book, each by Larry Burkett. Cost is $35, which includes shipping. The counseling is free, but the nonprofit Christian Financial Ministries asks that you share in the overhead costs with a modest donation each month. Contact numbers: 800-895-0512 or 678-797-9444 or www.good-steward.org.

- **Harbour Credit Counseling Services.** Jerry McTaggert says that Ray Noftsinger, the president of Harbour Credit Counseling, is a good man, and, Jerry highly recommends his nonprofit organization. Harbour Credit offers a similar debt management plan and has no application or setup fees. Contact numbers: 800-40 DEBTS, or 800-403-3287, or www.40debts.org.

As I mentioned, there are many fine organizations willing to help. If you want to find more Christian-based companies or something local, use your search engine or the Yellow Pages, looking under "Credit & Debt Counseling Services." One advantage to using a service like Christian Credit Counselors is that you never have to meet with anyone—it's all done over the phone. Whatever you do, be sure to choose an organization that uses an automatic pay-roll deduction service. It's better for everybody if you can't put your hands on the debt repayment money before it gets electronically shipped to your creditors.

Lots of Moonlight

There's another solution to paying off your credit card debts that some debt counselors ignore—earning some extra income.

We're talking volunteering for overtime, moonlighting with a second job, perhaps even having the wife work part-time outside the home while the kids are in school. I know that no one wants to hear, "Hey, why don't you work fifty or sixty hours to get out from underneath all that extra spending you did?" but when you get down to it, that's what you may have to do.

For the last twenty years, I've run a little tennis stringing business out of my home—and I've taught Nicole to string tennis rackets as well. There were some years when we were stringing thirty rackets a month, making ten dollars a racket. Sometimes that $300 a month was the difference between making it and not making it that month.

I also gave tennis lessons after my workday at Focus on the Family, teaching one or two hours starting at 5 P.M. The money was great, and it allowed us to keep Nicole at home raising the children during the day. Once the kids reached elementary and middle school, Nicole taught some tennis lessons as well.

There are lots of different things you can do. I hear that delivering pizza during dinnertime can be lucrative for the amount of time you put into it. Waiting tables one or two nights a week is a time-honored way to bring in some extra money. Maybe you did some house painting during the summer months when you were a college student and could paint on weekends. My church pastor told me that his father, a schoolteacher, sold shoes on Friday nights and Saturdays when times were tight. That's what families did in those days.

Extra money is not going to fly into your pocket. You have

to go out there and make it happen. Is there some "cottage" type industry that your wife can do from home? Is there a part-time job that she can take during the middle of the day while the kids are at school?

Sure, life would be better if you could come home from work, take your shoes off, and relax in the La-Z-Boy with a big iced tea and the newspaper. That's not going to happen, however, until you get off your duff and get that consumer debt paid off.

Sorry about that, but those are the consequences of spending more than you earn.

TEN

The Check-Out Lane

One of the ministries I support is called Second Chance, started by a young woman named Shawn Burns, who travels around the country speaking to young people about the importance of staying sexually pure before marriage.

You gotta love that. I became acquainted with Shawn after she spoke to my children's youth group about attending one of her "purity" camps that she puts on every summer. Although my teens never signed up, I believed in Shawn's fledgling ministry and asked to be put on her mailing list.

Second Chance is a small ministry—just Shawn and her volunteers—but I liked her pluckiness and willingness to swim against the cultural tide. With this background, I received an interesting letter in early 2000 from a friend of Shawn who said that Shawn had gotten into terrible financial trouble. She explained a little about Shawn's dire financial situation and appealed for my financial help.

I sent off a check and my best wishes for the future. Eighteen months passed before I ran into Shawn again. Naturally, I was curious about what happened and if she had turned things around on the financial front.

Shawn's story will encourage you as I bring this book to an end.

Shawn Burns grew up in sunny Southern California with a normal life that revolved around school, friends, and the beach. When she was seventeen, however, a grandmotherly woman in a Cadillac plowed into her boyfriend's car, causing moderate injuries to Shawn, who was sitting in the passenger's seat. Her boyfriend's insurance company picked up her $3,000 in medical fees but immediately filed a claim against the woman's insurance company, since the older woman was at fault.

It took a year for the two insurance companies to settle the claim, but in the end, Shawn's attorney received a small settlement, from which he was supposed to reimburse her boyfriend's insurance company. He failed to do that, however, nor did he inform Shawn that she had to pay back the $3,000 sum.

Shawn had a rude surprise two years later when she received a notice in the mail demanding a $3,000 payment. She asked her father what to do, and he said to call the attorney, who told her she could ignore that bill because it was "just a clause in the contract. They never really go after that money."

Shawn shrugged her shoulders and went on with life and began attending a school for chiropractics—an expensive proposition. By the time she graduated in 1991, she was responsible for $60,000 in student loans. Shawn began receiving the customary student loan bills following graduation, but when she inquired about a payment schedule, she was told by the nice people on the phone that she didn't have to pay them yet. *Don't worry about those student loans, Shawn. You have three years of deferment. We can wait.*

All this time, Shawn had no clue that the interest clock was ticking away. Her parents had never taught her about finances. She hadn't read any books about the topic. Her main creditor was telling her that she could pay her student loans when it suited her best. So she let things slide.

Meanwhile, seven years had passed since the original insurance company first asked to be paid back. They had not forgotten, and they sent Shawn a stinging letter stating that her debt had gone to "judgment," which meant that her debt was very much alive and now public record. Instead of owing $3,000, however, the amount had ballooned up to $10,000, thanks to high interest rates in the intervening seven years.

As for her $60,000 in student loans, Shawn always thought that she would be rolling in the dough "next year," but next year never came. As the original $60,000 increased each year due to interest, Shawn became more dispirited. She figured there was no way she could ever pay back such a large sum.

Besides, Shawn's heart was turning more to speaking to and working with teens about abstinence, so her chiropractic work had become a sideline. As she began devoting most of her waking hours to helping others, she heard a pastor say, "As long as you are in the ministry, you don't have to worry about things like money."

So Shawn let things slide further, even though she continued to receive damning letters and harassing phone calls from creditors, who made her feel like roadkill. She had to close out her bank accounts because one time her savings and checking accounts were garnished by the insurance company, who emptied them of $3,000—just about all the money she had saved. From then on, Shawn cashed her paychecks and paid her bills with money orders.

Shawn is not sure when her accumulation of bills reached a critical mass, but when Y2K rolled by, she learned that the $60,000 in student loans had morphed into a long-term debt of $106,000. That's what not making any payments for nine years will do to you. At that point, Shawn felt that her life had totally turned upside down. "I was in a spin, not able to see reality," she told me. "I felt complete hopelessness. Despair. I would crawl into bed in a fetal position and would want to sleep, but in order to fall asleep, I had to mentally go into denial and pretend that what was happening wasn't happening. I would tell myself that God would take care of it because I was involved in ministry, and since I was doing what he was telling me to do, everything was going to be all right. I completely shoved my problems into the back of the closet and shut the door."

A close friend named Valerie noticed that all was not right with Shawn. Valerie felt the prompting of the Holy Spirit to speak with Shawn, and she followed that leading. Like pealing the layers of an onion, it wasn't long before Valerie discovered Shawn's utter desperation. Valerie listened and then spoke the blunt truth: *God does not take care of your finances. You take care of them, and when you take care of your finances, then God will honor that and will work with you and your ministry.*

That evening in Valerie's home was the start of a long, long haul. Over the next few months, Shawn experienced the usual one step forward and two steps backward, and there were times when Shawn would become even more confused and helpless, causing her to ball up in a fetal position on her couch while Valerie encouraged her to grab the reins of her finances.

First things first. Valerie sat by while Shawn called her creditors to work out new repayment schedules. Often, Shawn spoke with belligerent people who verbally abused her with assorted insults and belittling statements. Whenever Shawn began to lose it, Valerie would step in and take the phone for her. As a third party, Valerie had the clarity to help Shawn deal with her creditors.

Next, Valerie helped Shawn map out an overall repayment plan—how much money she would allocate each month to this creditor, how much to that creditor, and so forth. Once a week, Valerie dropped by her apartment and patiently worked through the bills with Shawn, who wasn't allowed to touch her money. "Whatever is left over is what you can live on," said Valerie. This was tough love because sometimes there was only $15 left over for two weeks of food.

Valerie also found Shawn a regular job so that she could bring home a twice-monthly paycheck and counseled her to curb her teen ministry until she got back on her feet. Meanwhile, Valerie reminded her, "If you show God that you mean business, he will join you and make it happen."

Armed with a new attitude, Shawn meant business. She began working two jobs, and then she started working in a chiropractic office for a couple of days each week. She used her paychecks to chip away at her debts. The first to be paid off was the insurance company from that car accident long ago. Then there was a $1,200 court judgment for back taxes that had been hanging around like a springtime cold. That got paid. In just two years, she has reduced her $106,000 in student loans to less than $80,000. Shawn still has a long way to go before she is debt-free, but her future has never looked brighter.

"I'm not in bondage anymore," says Shawn. "I can remember when I would have a bill for $300, and I could hear the devil lying to me: *You don't have the money. You'll never have the money. You're hopeless.* So I listened and never made an attempt to pay the sum. Then I would walk by a shoe store and see a great sale price for a pair of shoes—$15. I would say to myself, 'What's $15?' But when you need food first, that $15 would not be a wise purchase. I learned that every little bit that I save toward paying off my debts shows good character and good-will. These days, I choose not to spend my money on things I don't really need because I'm choosing to pay my debts instead. That's why I'm not afraid anymore. I know God will provide if I'm a good steward."

––––––––––––––––

Wasn't that inspirational? What I like about Shawn's story is that it makes several strong points:

- **The feeling of denial is really strong.** We know how our minds work. We can talk ourselves into anything, even denying that our $10,000 credit card balance doesn't have to be repaid as fast as humanly possible. Are you in denial? Are you ignoring those big credit card balances because you find it easier to go through life that way?

- **Being in debt can cause you to freeze up.** Did you notice what Shawn said about feeling paralyzed by her debts?

Out-of-control debt can cause people not to think straight or act squarely. Examine your recent actions and ask yourself if you have done some things that were out of character, even for you. Ask your spouse, a parent, or a close friend the same question.

- **It helps to have friends (or counselors) available to help you see your problems and give you advice on what to do.** I'm serious. I hope this book is just the first step toward making a decision to tackle your debt head-on. Satan will whisper the same things into your mind that he told Shawn—that there's no way you can pay back what you owe, that you're worthless, and that your stupidity means that you don't deserve to be debt-free.

  Don't listen to the deceiver! When Shawn began listening to Valerie, it was better than being hooked up with a phone-a-friend lifeline. Valerie had the answers for Shawn. As for you, seek out friends and credit counselors who can help you navigate the shark-infested waters of debt.

- **You have to take the long haul.** You didn't overspend in one night, and you won't get out of debt overnight. It will take *years* to wipe out your crushing credit cards, but if you remain tenacious—and as focused as John Elway was when he started a ninety-nine-yard drive for the winning touchdown—you will eventually reach the goal line. Everyone I've talked to and all the research I've conducted say that the long, sustained effort to score on the Debt Defense was worth it.

- **Debt is expensive.** Maybe that $5,000 locked up in credit cards looks "manageable" today. But keep making minimum payments, keep letting that 18.3 percent interest stir the pot, and you have a recipe for the biggest humble pie of debt that you can ever imagine. Scripture is fairly blunt when describing those who have to borrow: "Just as the rich rule the poor, so the borrower is servant to the lender" (Proverbs 22:7). This verse doesn't mean you should never borrow money. It's just a friendly warning from the Lord that you should not make a loan without carefully examining your ability to pay for it. Until you can repay with the staggering interest rates on your debts, you are a servant to the banks that issued you the credit cards.

- **Paying off credit card debt is the best investment you'll ever make.** One way to keep yourself motivated about paying back your credit card debts is that it's a sure thing: you are saving hundreds and probably thousands of dollars in interest charges by paying off your debts early. Let's see you "earn" as much on Wall Street or through some mutual fund.

A Final Thought

We arrive at the critical juncture. It's time to wrap up *Real Solutions for Getting Out of Debt*. Are you going to put this book down and say, *You know, Mike made a pretty good speech, and I really should do something, but....*

You can fill in the blank with the excuse du jour. No matter how novel or how old, however, it is still an excuse.

Please, consider your financial future! Do something before it's too late! Take concrete steps today to lower your spending! Make a plan to pay off those credit cards!

Hopefully, I've equipped you with a better understanding of what debt is all about, given you plenty of ideas on how to save on everyday expenses, and offered real solutions for getting out of debt.

So, what are you going to do about it?